D1037708

MORE THAN PETTICOATS

Remarkable South Carolina Women

Lee Davis Perry

gpp®

Guilford, Connecticut

Text design by Nancy Freeborn
Map by Daniel Lloyd © Morris Book Publishing, LLC

Library of Congress Cataloging-in-Publication data is available on file.

ISBN 978-0-7627-4343-8

Printed in the United States of America
10 9 8 7 6 5 4 3 2 1

CONTENTS

South Carolina

INTRODUCTION

South Carolina's state motto is *Dum spiro, spero,* which, translated from the Latin, is, "While I breathe, I hope"—a statement that seems to perfectly capture the spirit of each of the remarkable women I came to know while researching and writing this book. Each of these fascinating individuals in some manner courageously hoped to foster some change for the better—be it in attitudes, living conditions, education, health care, or historic preservation. Some worked on a smaller scale within their own communities, and others branched out beyond their home cities and home state to make an impact nationally. All hoped for a better life for their own families and better lives for other families with the same struggles and hopes.

Sometimes the hopes and dreams of these visionary women were met with apathy and disdain due to sexism, racism, or both. Detractors often said that a woman's place was in the home and that stepping outside that sphere was unladylike and inappropriate. Each of these women displayed incredible tenacity in maintaining the poise and determination to do what she thought needed to be done, overcoming numerous obstacles and hardships along the way. As hard as it may be to comprehend today, women working outside the home to help support their own families, as Henrietta Johnston, Elizabeth Timothy, and Eliza Lucas Pinckney all did in the early days of the South Carolina colony, was a radical idea. Yes, altered personal circumstances led to each being thrust into that role. But they responded to the challenges with vigor, each preserving her family's welfare as well as earning a place of note in South Carolina's history.

Ann Pamela Cunningham, Lily Strickland Anderson, and Gertrude Sanford Legendre in turn all challenged the status quo of their day. They boldly and passionately tackled such "inappropriate" activities as fund-raising for historic preservation, composing and publishing music in a male-dominated field, and collecting museum specimens from remote and often dangerous destinations around the world. With steady resolve tempered by grace, each hoped to make a difference in her time and set a precedent for others to follow in the future.

The women of the Progressive Era had especially high hopes that they could reform the cultural and social makeup of the South's sleepy ways, and they ruffled a lot of feathers in their efforts to bring about change. From Laura Bragg's innovative museum programs that reached out to enlighten a broader public audience to Julia Peterkin's humanistic literary portrayals of African Americans based on her own experiences, new ground was crossed, and there was no turning back. Educators such as Wil Lou Gray and Septima Clark as well as Marie Cromer Seigler and Matilda Arabelle Evans compassionately toiled for years to improve the lives of South Carolinians and make lasting impacts in literacy, health care, and civil rights.

As I began my research into the many amazing stories from the history of South Carolina, I quickly found that the most difficult part of writing this book would be narrowing down the list of remarkable women to a reasonable group for inclusion. I endeavored to span the history of the state from its colonial settlement days through the twentieth century, incorporating women born before 1920—to suit the "More Than Petticoats" title. I attempted to cover various fields of interest, selecting only one artist, one writer, and one doctor, for example, from numerous interesting candidates within each field. I also wanted to feature women from different areas of the state since most were greatly influenced and challenged by their own immediate surroundings. I chose several women who are well known within our state's history and then selected some lesser-known women who I felt deserved more recognition for their achievements. The women in this collection represent a diversity of economic, educational, social, and racial backgrounds, proving that significant change can germinate in any circumstances if the will is there. With these caveats in mind, I hope that these women's stories may give some insight into the dynamic lives of a cross section of South Carolina women and spur further study of other outstanding women in our state and our nation.

Finally, in researching the lives of these women, I often encountered different versions of the "facts." As is often the case in the recording of events, different sources may have different recollections of the same event. In most such cases I have chosen what I thought would be more interesting or engaging in the telling of each woman's life. My goal was to convey the essence of their lives and perhaps bring some long overdue attention to their accomplishments largely neglected in the recounting of our state's history. I hope, too, that this book and others in Globe Pequot's *More Than Petticoats* series will inspire readers young and old to lead remarkable lives that embrace the spirit of *Dum spiro, spero*.

HENRIETTA DERING JOHNSTON

ca. 1674-1729

America's First Female Artist

A PROMISING LIFE IN THE NEW WORLD beckoned for the Johnstons as they set sail for Charles Town in the Carolina colony. After leaving England, the first stop was the Madeira Islands, where Reverend Gideon Johnston disembarked for fresh provisions, only to miss the ship as it weighed anchor with his family aboard. Despite this less than auspicious start, Gideon and his wife, Henrietta, hoped for a better life as he assumed his duties as commissary for the bishop of London and rector of St. Philip's Church. Eventually securing passage on another ship, Gideon arrived outside Charles Town harbor some six months after departing England.

The ship waited for an incoming tide to bring her safely into her docking berth. Gideon, impatient and anxious to learn his family's fate, joined two other men, a merchant and a sailor, going ashore immediately on a small boat. Unable to fight the currents, they were swept over to a small island where Gideon and the merchant were stranded for twelve agonizing days without food or fresh water. After three days, the sailor who had accompanied

Henrietta Johnston's portrait (1711) presents a lovely image of the young girl, Henriette Charlotte Chastaigner (Mrs. Nathaniel Broughton, 1700–1754).

them attempted to swim to another island to look for help and was drowned. Numerous vessels were sent out to search for the missing passengers when finally "a Canoo got to us when we were at the last Gasp and just upon the point of Expiring, and Next Morning we were conveyed to the Port of the Continent where I lay a Fortnight before I cou'd recover Strength enough to reach the Town." In fact the exposure to the elements had left Reverend Johnston with severe sunburn, "fever and ague, and the dry belly ack" so that he was to become a virtual invalid for the next nine months. To add to his duress, the expenses of the search parties were charged to Johnston, and his distraught, young wife met him with more bad news when they were finally reunited.

Little is known about the early life of Henrietta Johnston, including the date and place of her birth. It is believed that she was born in Quintin near Rennes in Northern France around 1674 to French Huguenot parents, Francis and Suzanna de Beaulieu. Henrietta and her sister, Ann, immigrated with them to London in 1687, perhaps to escape religious persecution. The Huguenots, French Protestants, had lost their right to religious freedom in Catholic-dominated France with the revocation of the Edict of Nantes in 1685. Many fled their native country to seek religious tolerance in other nations such as England, Ireland, Holland, and the American colonies, particularly Charles Town (now Charleston) in South Carolina.

Details of Henrietta's adult life remain obscure as well. Parish records show her family's affiliation with St. Martin-in-the-Fields Anglican Church in London and also document her marriage to her first husband, Robert Dering, in 1694 at his parish church in Knightsbridge, also in the London area. Dering was born at Surrendon Dering, the family estate in Kent County, England, on April 13, 1669. He was a member of a large, well-established English family who held strong ties to the monarchy. Robert's father, Sir

Edward Dering, was a former member of Parliament. He served on the commission for the Act of Settlement for Ireland and was one of three commissioners of the Privy Seal for the crown. These political connections were to benefit Henrietta's professional career later as her life unfolded.

Within the first years of their marriage, Henrietta and Robert moved to Ireland. Two of Robert's brothers held prominent appointments there—Charles as auditor of the Irish Exchequer, and Daniel as a colonel in the British Army serving in Ireland— and may have influenced the couple's decision to settle there too. Two daughters were born to them, one of whom was named Mary. (Mary later became a lady-in-waiting for the daughters of King George II, carrying on the family tradition of links to the crown.) Robert died sometime between 1698 and 1702, leaving Henrietta a young widow.

After Robert's death Henrietta stayed in Ireland and, possibly as a means of support, made pastel portraits of many of the Dering family's friends and relatives—English gentry with important positions in Ireland. Fortuitously, nine pastels from this time period surfaced at an auction of the contents of an eighteenth-century Irish country house, Belvedere, as recently as 1980. Six of these revealed artist signatures similar to one inscribed "Henrietta Dering Fecit/ Dublin Anno 1705" on the wooden backing of another portrait. Many inscriptions of this kind have survived through the years on the majority of her existing work, confirming her as the artist and providing the location and date of rendering, allowing her artistic career to be traced.

Several theories abound about her training, without much consensus from art scholars. A French-born woman was an unlikely candidate for formal art training in Dublin, strictly controlled by the Guild of Painters and Stainers. She may have been largely self-taught by studying and copying the Dering's family portrait collection and perhaps guided from time to time by a painter working for them. Her use of pastels, which were not widely used in her day, also adds to the mystery. Her pastel crayons must have suited her well, however, allowing her to use a soft touch on a smaller scale, with most portraits measuring less than 12 inches square. Compared to the difficulties of carrying large canvasses and oil paints, pastels would have been easy to carry to the homes of her sitters.

According to the register of St. Andrew's Parish, Dublin, Henrietta remarried on April 11, 1705, this time to a clergyman named Gideon Johnston. It was a second marriage for Johnston as well. He had two sons, James and Robert, who were about ten and eight years old, respectively. Gideon Johnston's background was less privileged than that of Henrietta's first husband. He was the son of the Reverend James Johnston, "a poor clergyman gentleman." Gideon's early life began about 1668 in Loony, County Mayo, Ireland. In 1692 he was graduated from Trinity College in Dublin. He became a clergyman in the Diocese of Killala and Anchrony and, at the time of his marriage to Henrietta, was the vicar of Castlemore.

He was officiating at Tuam Cathedral in 1707 when he and Henrietta made the decision to immigrate to South Carolina so that he could become a missionary in the Province. Reverend Johnston, who had a very favorable reputation for diligence and ability, had heard of the great need for ministers in the colonies and felt the call. The family of six (plus four or five additional dependents) began preparations by traveling to London in early 1707 to apply to The Society for the Propagation of the Gospel in Foreign Parts, a missionary division of the Church of England, for an appointment. The appointment was slow in coming, and the family's financial reserves were depleted as they waited for many months on a decision.

Finally, in November 1707, the appointment came for commissary of the Church of England in North Carolina, South Carolina, and the Islands of the Bahamas. Reverend Johnston would also become minister of St. Philip's Church in Charles Town, to fill a recent opening. Now the real preparations began as the family attempted to find the funds to make the trip. Fortunately, the bishop of London lent some support, and the Society granted Reverend Johnston fifty pounds for his expenses, "he giving security that he will take the first opportunity of conveying himself and Family to Charlestown." Within a month the perilous voyage began. After Reverend Johnston's misstep in Madeira he had waited six months to be reunited with his family—only to be stranded on a small island for nearly two weeks just outside Charles Town harbor.

When the rescued but exhausted and ill Reverend Johnston finally reached Charles Town, Henrietta related that he would not be welcomed as the new rector of St. Philip's nor was the family able to take up residence in the rectory promised to him. Another clergyman from Maryland had usurped his position, managing to get himself elected rector by the parishioners a year before the Johnstons arrived. Reverend Richard Marsden was already officiating and occupying the rectory. For four long months the Johnston family hung on by borrowing money from the Provincial treasury as an advance on Gideon's salary and living in a rented house "which was twice broke open, and robbed of several things." Their situation couldn't have gotten much worse in this unfamiliar land with no church of their own and no support from the congregation they had come to serve. Henrietta also battled poor health as she contracted the fevers that were so widespread in the malarial port city while attempting to care for and encourage her husband and children. With quill pen in hand, she wrote letters dictated by her crippled husband pleading to the bishop for a return to England.

My Lord, I never repented so much of anything, my Sins excepted, as my coming to this Place, nor has ever Man been treated with less humanity and Compassion considering how much I had suffered in my Passage, than I have been since my Arrival in it.

Not only were Reverend Johnston's professional hopes dashed but also Charles Town proved to be vastly different from what he had heard about it while in London. Tales of ". . . the goodness of the climate, the fertility of the soil, the plenty of all things necessary for the life of man, the peaches, the apricots, the nectarines, with super-abundance . . . " had made him eager to transplant his family. But in 1708 Charles Town, settled less than thirty years earlier, was still a raw seaport under constant threat from the Indians outside the town's fortress walls and the sinister pirates lurking just offshore. The 3,500 inhabitants of the town were an agitated mix of sailors, merchants, pirates, planters, Indian traders, indentured servants, African and Indian slaves, and others hoping to profit (either legitimately or otherwise) from the bustling, chaotic environment of the crude settlement.

By the end of September the family's fate finally improved. Reverend Marsden resigned from St. Philip's and relocated to a nearby parish. Reverend Johnston was installed as the new minister, and the family moved into the rectory, a "good brick house, with gardens and a plantation, two Negro slaves and a stock of cattle" located just outside the city's walls. But even with his newly improved circumstances, Reverend Johnston continued to rail against the people of Charles Town as well as his own parishioners in his letters to England.

I cannot be over fond of staying in such a place and amongst such a strange sort of people, especially where the salary is so small. The People here, generally speaking, are the Vilest race of Men upon the Earth; they have neither honour, nor honesty nor Religion enough to entitle them to any tolerable Character . . . and are the most factious and seditious people in the Whole World.

His criticisms specifically named the religious dissenters and non-Anglicans such as the Presbyterians, Baptists, Congregationalists, and Quakers who were quite unhappy about the Anglican Church's stronghold over the colony.

Notably absent from Johnston's critique were the French Huguenots, many of whom had befriended the family, possibly through Henrietta's Huguenot ancestry, assisting them during their rocky start as missionaries in the New World. Among them were a fellow student from Trinity College, the Reverend Dr. Francis de Jau of the nearby Goose Creek community, and the Reverend Paul L'Escot, minister of the Huguenot Church in Charles Town. Other friendships were established with "Messrs. St. Julien, Le Noble, and Mazeick." Dr. John Thomas, a Huguenot who had treated the family for their numerous ailments without accepting payment, was praised as "the only P'son that deserves the Name of a Phisician in this place." Dr. Thomas "has been extremely kind and generous to me," Reverend Johnston wrote.

These friendships held significance in another respect as well. Throughout their ordeal, Henrietta had continued her work as a portraitist, and the wives and daughters of these men were the subjects of many of Henrietta's portraits, considered some of her most outstanding work. Susanne LeNoble, Mademoiselle Cramahe, Mrs. Paul Mazyck, and Mrs. Nathaniel Broughton (whose portrait is shown earlier in this chapter) were among those ladies of French ancestry whom she drew while living in Charles Town. Portraits of Dr. Thomas's stepdaughters, Mary, Judith, and Anne DuBose, were perhaps rendered in appreciation of his medical services to her family. Other subjects were members of her husband's congregation at St. Philip's such as

Colonel William Rhett, a local hero who had successfully captured the notorious pirate Stede Bonnett, who was depicted in a dignified fashion befitting his status, wearing velvet and silk under a breastplate of armor and donning an elaborate, long wig.

Stylistically, in Henrietta's American portraits the female subjects usually wore thin, white chemises under simple dresses, and the males were depicted in street clothes with wigs; their posture is erect with the head slightly turned toward the viewer. A distinctive feature of her portraits is the large, oval, expressive eyes that dominate the sitter's face. Typically, she posed her subjects for bust-style portraits, showing the head and shoulders and allowing her to omit full-length arms and hands that were not her strong suit. Her technique changed subtly in her new surroundings. The colonial portraits reflected her domestic circumstances in their simplicity, and they were slightly smaller and more pale and delicate, with minimalist backgrounds, than those done in Ireland. All these features suggest the careful conservation of her hard-to-obtain art materials, which had to be imported at great cost. Perhaps it was also necessary for her to complete the work quicker due to her responsibilities as a housewife, mother, and wife to the ailing and provoked minister of one of the most important Anglican congregations of the colonies. Perhaps a completed commission resulted in faster payment as well.

In response to his mounting debts and the often delayed payments of his salary, Reverend Johnston acknowledged the importance of his wife's contribution to the family's survival in a letter to the Society in 1709, "Were it not for the assistance my wife gives me by drawing pictures . . . I shou'd not have been able to live." This passing reference to Henrietta gives validation that she was compensated for her portraits, making her the earliest professional female artist in America. Unfortunately, by July 1710 another letter stated, "My wife who greatly helped me, by drawing pictures, has long ago made an end of her materials."

In April 1711 Henrietta made a return trip to England with multiple objectives. She was hoping to improve her health, purchase much-needed drawing supplies, and hand-deliver petitions from the local clergy to the Society to grant them more compensation. Having borrowed more funds from friends for her travel expenses, Reverend Johnston stayed behind in Charles Town, unable to accompany her, in compliance with a law that prevented debtors from leaving the province. Shortly after Henrietta's departure, initial reports came back to Charles Town that her ship, the *Loyal Johnson,* had been captured by pirates off the coast of Virginia. Gideon was completely distraught, but weeks later he learned that the ship had escaped its would-be captors, and Henrietta was able to reach London. While there she must have been quite busy with clerical conferences, visits to the school where her stepson James was a student (sponsored by the Society at his father's urgent request), and taking advantage of opportunities to continue her artistic pursuits. A couple of portraits from her visit survive and suggest that she may have worked to help support herself while in England.

Eventually, Henrietta's appeals to the Society in London were successful. Her husband was given the additional appointment of Missionary of the Society with an allowance of fifty pounds per year, and a curate and schoolmaster were funded to assist him in his duties. He was also granted a gift of thirty pounds "as a further Consideration of the Great Services pains and Losses" that he had endured.

By late 1712 Henrietta returned to Charles Town only to find Gideon ever-determined to leave the city despite his improved situation. Still struggling with poor health, he made a trip back to England in March 1713 with funds raised by his colleagues. More than two years passed before his health allowed him to go back to his family (and perhaps his reluctance to return to his duties in

Charles Town also contributed to the delay). Once again he arrived to a city full of difficulties. The Yemassee Indian War had erupted nearby and had filled the town with refugees. Many of these had sought shelter in his rectory, and Henrietta was coping as best she could to manage the overflowing household. Two destructive hurricanes had struck Charles Town in 1713 and 1714, the latter severely damaging the new St. Philip's Church that was under construction as well as the Johnstons' home. Food and clothing were even scarcer commodities.

Somehow, amidst the chaos, Henrietta was able to continue her drawings. Her portraits from this time depict calm and elegant subjects among her friends and their children. Possibly her work may have been a brief escape from her arduous duties at home. Gideon, as his health continued to deteriorate, was less and less involved in the problems of his church and still hoped to return to England permanently. But this was not to be. One day in April 1716 he joined a group of prominent men on a sloop escorting the Governor who was boarding a ship bound for England. As the sloop left the departing ship "a gust of wind . . . oversett" the sloop "this side our Barr about four or five Leagues from Land; they all escaped by Singular Providence but Mr. Commissary (Johnston), who through weakness of Body could not come out of the Hold and was drowned there." Weeks passed before the sloop and the remains of his body were found "on the same Bank of Land on which he was near perishing at his first arrival in the Country," according to a contemporary account by the Reverend William T. Bull.

Local clergy sent a letter to the Bishop in London telling of the tragedy. They beseeched his "Goodness in the behalf of Mr. Commissaryes Widow, four children and family, left in great Affliction and in Deplorable Circumstances." It is not known how he responded or how the family fared in the years following Gideon's death. But signed and dated portraits reveal that Henrietta continued to work in Charles Town and even made a trip in 1725 to New York, where she completed at least five pastels. By 1726 she was back in Charles Town as two unidentified male portraits were dated then. Three years later on March 9, 1729, she died and was buried in St. Philip's churchyard.

Although there is but limited information about Henrietta's life that can be pieced together through church records, Gideon's correspondence with London that chronicles their life, and her signed portraiture, it is important to acknowledge this early colonial South Carolina lady as America's first professional female painter and the first American pastellist.

Approximately fifty of Henrietta's portraits are known to exist in private collections in Ireland and the United States and in American museums including the Gibbes Museum of Art, Greenville County Museum of Art, Museum of Early Southern Decorative Arts, and the Metropolitan Museum of Art, attesting to her importance to American art.

ELIZABETH ANN TIMOTHY

ca. 1700-1757

America's First Female Publisher

Whereas the late Printer of this Gazette hath been deprived of his Life . . . I take this Opportunity of informing the Publick, that I shall continue the said Paper as usual; and hope, by the Assistance of my Friends, to make it as entertaining and correct as may be reasonably expected. Wherefore I flatter my self, that all those Persons, who by Subscription or otherwise, assisted my late Husband, in the Prosecution of the said Undertaking, will be kindly pleased to continue their Favours and good Offices to his poor afflicted Widow and six small Children and another hourly expected.

THIS NOTICE APPEARED IN THE *South Carolina Gazette* published in Charlestown, South Carolina, on January 4, 1739. It was signed by Elizabeth Ann Timothy, thus noting the beginning of her career as the first woman in the colonies to publish a newspaper. Although the masthead stated that the *Gazette* was "Printed by Peter Timothy" (her son), Elizabeth Timothy had assumed the full duties of publisher of the newspaper in a time when few women even

This artist's sketch offers an interpretation of Elizabeth Timothy as she penned articles for the *South Carolina Gazette*.

worked outside of the home. Her husband, Lewis Timothy, had died suddenly only the month before, in what the *Gazette* described as "an unhappy Accident," leaving Elizabeth the sole supporter of her family of young children. Fortunately, her background had prepared her to take on the challenge of her inherited career.

Although little is known of her early life, Elizabeth was born in Holland around the year 1700 and was raised by a family who gave her an education for girls that included "knowledge of accounts." She married Louis Timothée, a French Huguenot whose father had fled to Holland when many French Protestants left France in the wake of religious persecution after the revocation of the Edict of Nantes in 1685. In turn, Louis and Elizabeth emigrated from Rotterdam, Holland, to Philadelphia, Pennsylvania, to pursue opportunities in the New World. Documents include them in the list of foreigners on the ship *Brittania* of London, Michael Franklin, Master. On September 21, 1731, Louis took the oath of allegiance to King George II of England, becoming a British subject in the Pennsylvania Province. The oath was required for all males over the age of sixteen who had not officially obtained permission from the crown to emigrate to the colonies. At that time the Timothée family comprised his wife, Elizabeth, and their four children, Peter, Louis, Charles, and Mary, ranging in age from six down to one.

Soon after their arrival in Pennsylvania, an advertisement appeared in Benjamin Franklin's *Pennsylvania Gazette:* "This is to give Notice that Mr. Louis Timothée, Master of the French Tongue, hath settled himself with his family in this City, in order to keep a publick French School; he will also, if required, teach the said Language to any young Gentlemen or Ladies, at their Lodgings." It seems that his multiple linguistic abilities as well as a proficiency in the printing business, which he had learned in Holland, led to an association with Benjamin Franklin. Franklin, ever the enterprising entrepreneur, was interested in starting a foreign-language newspaper aimed at the large German-speaking population settled in Pennsylvania. With Timothée as editor, he published the first issue of the *Philadephische Zeitung* on May 6, 1732. Within the paper, Timothée stated that the new periodical would be published weekly, once three hundred subscribers were secured. By June 24, 1732, the second issue announced that fifty subscribers were signed on and that the newspaper would print every fortnight. Unfortunately, no additional copies have been found, which suggests that the trial publication did not survive to publish more editions.

Despite the failure of the foreign-language paper, Franklin must have been favorably impressed by Louis Timothée. Recognizing his scholarly abilities and perhaps hoping to aid Timothée by supplementing his family's income, Franklin recommended him for the position of librarian of the Philadelphia Library Company. Timothée signed articles of agreement with the Library Company on November 14, 1732. His compensation was one pound sterling per month as well as any additional "reasonable reward" that the library directors might bestow. Timothée also was employed by Franklin at this time as a journeyman printer. Timothée's initial contract to serve as librarian was for a period of three months, but he continued in the position for a full year until new opportunities presented by his benefactor, Benjamin Franklin, lured him away from Philadelphia. (Franklin himself filled the position of librarian for the Philadelphia Library Company after Timothée's resignation.)

Upon the death of the publisher of the *South Carolina Gazette* in September 1733, Franklin quickly formed a partnership with Timothée to take over the newspaper and printing business in Charlestown by November 1733, similar to other arrangements with other partners in cities throughout the colonies. The agreement identified him as "Lewis Timothée of the said City Printer (now bound on a voyage to Charlestown in South Carolina)" and specified a term of six years. Franklin furnished him "with a press and letters, on an agreement of partnership, by which I was to receive one-third of the profits of the business, paying one-third of the expense." In the event of Timothée's death, a provision was made for his son to continue the business:

> . . . if Peter Timothée son of the said Lewis Timothée shall be capable of carrying on and will carry on the Business of printing . . . as it ought to be carried on . . . It shall be in the power of the said Peter Timothée to keep and improve the materials of

printing so provided by the said Benjamin Franklin . . . until the Term of Copartnership . . . is expired.

Timothée arrived in Charlestown in late fall and resumed weekly publication of the *South Carolina Gazette* on February 2, 1734 in a shop on Church Street. Elizabeth remained in Philadelphia to settle his affairs and oversee the moving of their household. Franklin's business journal noted that he had "adjusted accounts with Mrs. Timothy" on March 26, 1734, after which she and the children followed her husband to Charlestown.

Anticipating the lack of local news items to fill the pages while getting the paper up and running, Timothée brought with him essays, poetry, and news from other colonial newspapers and from British journals. He also assumed the role of official printer for the provincial government, and on February 26, 1734, the Commons House journal entry specifies a payment to him of ninety-six pounds for "printing several Copys of the Militia and other Laws several Trading Bonds and advertisements &c." He also undertook printing his most ambitious project, Judge Nicholas Trott's *Laws of the Province of South Carolina.*

Timothée maintained a close relationship with his mentor, Franklin, and bought books and printing supplies from him on a regular basis. Franklin's accounts show purchases by Timothée of five hundred almanacs in November 1734, five hundred more in 1735, and three hundred in 1737. Some of the other popular titles he bought in quantity from Franklin included "100 Every Man his own Dr.," "6 doz primmers," "100 Catechism," and "6 Mason Books." Fulfilling other colonial residents' needs, he sold ink powder, sealing wax, quills, and writing paper. He operated a book bindery and printed a variety of legal forms including leases and releases, bills of sale, mortgages, apprentice indentures, bills of lading, and powers of attorney, among others. His first imprint was a twenty-four-page pamphlet, *An Essay on Currency,* in April 1734, followed by many others on a diverse array of topics. His high standard of print quality was evident in all of his endeavors.

Timothée's position as official printer for the colony required a high degree of skill as well as civic duty. In those days of limited, slow communication, the printing office was a point of contact with the outside world and thus was responsible for diligent and earnest attempts at accurate and reliable information. Timothée seems to have embraced this obligation and immersed himself and his wife in the life of the community. He anglicized the spelling of his name to "Lewis Timothy" and became one of the founders and officers of the South Carolina Society, a social and charitable organization. He helped organize a subscription postal system that originated at his printing office, which probably also benefited his newspaper's circulation. He obtained a land grant in 1736 for six hundred acres and one town lot in Charlestown. His monopoly on official printing was a lucrative venture revealed in the Commons House records showing 2,146 pounds sterling due to him for copies of Trott's *Laws* and other documents.

On the other hand, Timothy's *Gazette* subscribers were often slow in payment, and he had a large family to support. Even with the unfortunate death of one child in Philadelphia and another in Charleston, they were a family of eight. He published a plea to his delinquent subscribers:

> whereas several of my Subscribers have constantly taken but never paid me . . . I must again request them to consider, that as they would take it ill of me, if I should neglect them one Week, it certainly must be unpleasant and discouraging to me not to receive my quarterly or least yearly Payment.

After his death in December 1738 this problem would continue to plague his widow as well.

For five years Elizabeth led the behind-the-scenes but demanding life of a woman whose husband was diligently trying to get ahead and establish himself in a bustling colonial community. Charlestown was a thriving port city but had plenty of competition in Timothy's chosen field of publishing and printing. With his death, his capable but inexperienced wife faced the prospect of trying to support her large family. Taking over the management of the *South Carolina Gazette* as well as the printing business would not only provide for her family but also protect her oldest son's interest in his father's business until he came of age as set forth in the contract with Benjamin Franklin. She did not hesitate to step up to the challenge.

The business was in relatively good shape except for the casual way in which records and accounts were kept. As Franklin wrote of Lewis Timothy, "He was a man of learning, and honest but ignorant in matters of account; and tho' he sometimes made me remittances, I could get no account from him, nor any satisfactory state of our partnership while he lived." In the course of settling her husband's estate, Elizabeth immediately inserted an advertisement in the *Gazette* revealing the business and personal duress she must have felt. In the ad she stated that she was "under an absolute Necessity of settling all her said Husband's Accounts . . . in which she hath been much retarded by Sickness, as well of herself as her Family; and as many of the outstanding Debts are but small, she hopes no Persons will lay her under a Necessity of putting them to any charge in the Recovery thereof." To compound her difficulties, she tragically lost two of her sons to the "sickness" later in the year—Charles in September and Joseph in October 1739.

Elizabeth Timothy's first year of control of the newspaper reflects her inexperience in journalism and publishing, and perhaps her distractions as she struggled to care for her family at the same time. During the 1730s and 1740s, the physical makeup of the newspaper consisted of four pages approximately eight inches wide by thirteen inches deep. The type was set in two columns. Typically, the format of the newspaper had devoted the front page to foreign and domestic news gathered from other periodicals along with local official proclamations. The second page was made up of one column of local news, letters to the editor, and features such as the list of ships in port, commodities prices, export statistics, and descriptions of runaway slaves. The third page usually featured an original essay or poem to engage the reader's interest, and the fourth contained the advertising. Just as her husband first resorted to when reorganizing the paper, she tapped into editorial material from other colonial papers and British journals as a substitute for seeking out local news items or original literary work.

Advertising and subscriptions were the two main sources of income for the *Gazette*. Fortunately, advertising revenues stayed consistent during this first year despite the dearth of original content. The normal ad size was one column wide and two inches deep, and it cost one pound. The ad could run in the paper three times for this rate, but the size and number of insertions was often flexible with considerable leeway given. For a period of time, official advertising was allowed and was profitable to the *Gazette* as well as other papers. The Commons House journal documents a payment of fifty-six pounds and fifteen shillings in 1740 to Elizabeth Timothy for "printing Proclamations, Abstracts of Acts of the General Assembly, and Advertisements inserted in the *South Carolina Gazette*." Although no circulation records exist, the newspaper generally had good support, but often subscribers were slow to pay their fee of three pounds annually. This was a common problem pervasive among colonial printers. Like her husband before her, Elizabeth was forced to advertise frequently for the payment of delinquent accounts. In 1742 she warned her subscribers that she was employing persons to collect from those who "owe from three to Eight Years."

On the printing side of the business Elizabeth initially attempted fewer imprints, therefore less income from them was received. However, she did not appear to shrink from controversy in her selection of topics. During the 1739 yellow fever epidemic ravaging Charlestown, she continued publishing pamphlets about the inoculation debate, a new and mostly untested practice at the time. By 1740 religious discussions surrounding the popular but controversial Irish Reverend George Whitefield's visits to Charlestown stimulated the production of more imprints to meet the demand for this material. When young Charlestown native Eliza Lucas succeeded in planting indigo as a viable crop in the colonies, Elizabeth promoted an imprint, "Instructions on the Cultivation of Indigo." As her confidence and skill grew, the newspaper attained more credibility. The *Gentleman's Magazine* in England often relied upon the *South Carolina Gazette* as one of its primary sources of colonial news. Benjamin Franklin also reprinted many of these first "lady publisher" articles in Philadelphia. While Peter Timothy matured and worked alongside his mother, she edited a lively and interesting newspaper full of the "freshest advices, foreign and domestic."

Eventually, Elizabeth was able to lend a more businesslike approach to the enterprise than her husband had done. Franklin praised her industry and efficiency in his autobiography when he wrote:

> . . . she not only sent me as clear a state as she could find of the transactions past, but continued to account with greatest regularity and exactness every quarter afterwards, and managed the business with such success, that she not only brought up reputably a family of children, but, at the expiration of the term, was able to purchase of me the printing-house, and establish her son in it.

With Peter firmly in charge, she completely relinquished her responsibilities of editor and printer to him in 1746. Elizabeth set up and operated a book and stationery shop next door to the printing office, then located on King Street. She advertised "Pocket Bibles, Primmers, Horn Books, Dyche's spelling books, *Reflections on Courtship and Marriage,* Armstrong's *Poem on Health,* the *Westminster Confession of Faith,* Watt's *Psalms and Hymns,* and the popular *Poor Richard's* and *Pocket Almanacks.*" Again, most of these titles were those purchased regularly from the family's friend Benjamin Franklin.

By the time of her death in 1757, Elizabeth Timothy's will reflected that her endeavors on behalf of her family had been quite successful. She left her business interests, as well as a silver watch that had belonged to her late husband, to her son with instructions that it be passed down to her grandson. To her daughter Mary Elizabeth, she left a small tract of land, a house on King Street, two slaves, and half of her clothing and furniture. To her daughter Catherine, she left a house and three slaves, and to her daughter Louisa, the remainder of her estate including a house, three slaves, and furniture.

Her legacy also included a strong foundation of high standards in journalism and integrity for the family business, which went on to foster her son's influential leadership through the Revolutionary period and the formation of the new nation. During Peter Timothy's tenure the *South Carolina Gazette* was considered one of the best and most effective Whig newspapers in the southern colonies. Among other active political roles, he held the position of clerk of the General Assembly, which drafted the new constitutional government. Subsequently he was imprisoned by the British in St. Augustine, Florida, during the war. Upon his accidental death later in 1782, his wife, Ann, following in her mother-in-law's footsteps, became the *Gazette*'s publisher and proprietor of the book shop. In turn, her son, Benjamin Franklin Timothy, carried on the family enterprise into the early years of the nineteenth century.

ELIZA LUCAS PINCKNEY

1722-1793

Innovative Planter and Matriarch

SIXTEEN-YEAR-OLD ELIZA LUCAS and her younger sister Polly accompanied their parents as they set sail for her father's newly inherited estate along Wappoo Creek near the Ashley River outside Charlestown. Like many other families arriving in the colony, they had come from the British island of Antigua in the West Indies, where a plantation economy flourished and where trade was not only a lively mix of goods but also of people and ideas. Antigua's main cash crop was sugar, a commodity that made the island a valuable link in the shipping routes between England, Africa, and America. But, even though her father's holdings in Antigua were substantial among the sugar planters, many factors such as the fluctuations in the world market, interest rates, weather, competition, and the quality of the sugarcane crop contributed to a volatile situation, at best, for the family's fortunes. Growing up close to her father, Eliza often listened as he discussed the ups and downs of the business. George Lucas was closely acquainted with the vulnerability of a single crop economy, and his young daughter grasped the inherent difficulties. So she was not too surprised when he announced to his family in 1739 that they would move to another English colony, the province of South Carolina, to live on the property left to him by his father, John Lucas.

The elder Lucas had acquired the land in 1713 as an investment from which he could harvest timber and other provisions for support of his endeavors in the West Indies. To this property, George added two more plantations along the Carolina coast, Waccamaw on the river of the same name and Garden Hill on the Combahee River. He hoped to try his luck on these new lands with the promise of lower interest rates and the option to diversify his crops. Still desiring to align himself with Mother England, he traveled there to purchase a major's commission in the Thirty-Eighth Regiment of Foot, First Battalion, South Staffordshire Regiment. Based in Antigua, this regiment was part of the regular British Army, which gave Lucas some stature and identity with Britain.

In keeping with the custom of the day, George Lucas believed that a proper education for boys necessitated boarding school in England, and Eliza's two younger brothers had been sent there at an early age without question. Girls' schooling was traditionally a more modest effort, and daughters were often taught at home in subject matter that focused on needlework, music, and the classics. Departing from the norm, George Lucas sent Eliza to England for her studies. For about five years, from around 1732 to 1738, Eliza Lucas received a far more practical education than girls of her age usually did. Her studies incorporated math, bookkeeping, British history, literature, geography, and botany. As England's empire grew, some realized that the high mortality rate in foreign lands could leave many women as well as young men assuming the responsibilities of their families' businesses and estates. Progressive parents believed it was better to prepare both sons and daughters with an education that emphasized the importance of an orderly and structured environment approached in a regular and methodical way.

Another key element to success in this early global economy was communication through businesslike correspondence. The art of letter writing demonstrating a command of the English language while employing the powers of persuasion and salesmanship led to greater gains in the world of commerce. Eliza's writing style reflected early training in this art and was notable for the absence of a young person's gossip and what she considered "giddy gaiety" or frivolous activity that "waists our time." Wasting time was not to be a luxury in her future.

The family's emigration from Antigua to Carolina took place soon after Eliza's return from school in England. She met the change with a spirit of adventure, albeit with a bit of reluctance as well. However, soon after their arrival she was captivated by the rich flora and fauna of the Carolina Lowcountry. The ancient live oaks with their widespread boughs draped with silvery moss and the fragrant yellow Jessamine vine tumbling about enchanted her. Plantation life seemed to hold new promise for Eliza and her family. Even her frail mother, who had suffered from the unending heat in Antigua, hoped to improve her health a bit with the milder climate. And for this fair-haired, delicate-featured teenager, the excitement of Charlestown was close by just waiting for exploration. Charlestown was a vibrant port city bustling with activity as ships carrying luxury goods, supplies, and new settlers arrived regularly. A society based on English traditions was emerging, and Eliza looked forward to joining in the social gatherings of teas and parties and meeting other young people. As a daughter of a planter she had hopes of marrying one day into one of the other wealthy planter families, as was the norm for a well-born girl in the plantation south of the 1730s.

All this changed abruptly one day when her father summoned her for a talk. He held a letter he had received from the office of Antigua's Royal Governor. It stated that by order of the King of England he was to return to his military regiment in the West Indies—immediately. He faced an important decision. He had only begun to instruct his slaves in the clearing and development of the land into a viable rice-growing venture, a crop that was already yielding great riches for many Lowcountry planters. Successful rice cultivation required vast fields irrigated at specific intervals through a system of dikes and floodgates. Major alterations to the landscape such as clearing much heavily wooded terrain and constructing the dikes and gates were necessary before the rice could be planted. Much labor-intensive work was still ahead. After a brief deliberation he decided to entrust his eldest daughter with the responsibility of not only caring for his sickly wife and his youngest daughter but also the "business of three plantations," including a large number of slaves. He would stay in close correspondence with her from his post in Antigua, but Eliza would be in charge of the family fortunes in Carolina. A bit taken aback, Eliza listened carefully as her father offered that if she needed help before a letter could reach him, she should consult with the owners of the neighboring plantations, Mr. Charles Pinckney or Mr. Andrew Deveaux. They were experienced rice planters and would certainly share their counsel from time to time.

As her father set sail to answer his military obligation, Eliza must have felt a heavy weight of responsibility. A carefree life of social engagements and possible courtship would have to be put on hold while she tackled the monumental tasks before her. Now the "practical education" that her father had supported was going to be tested, and she didn't want to let him or her family down. Soon she settled into a structured routine of rising before dawn, inspecting the plantation and discussing the day's work ahead in the rice fields with the overseer. Her afternoons were taken up by detailed letters she composed to her father reporting on the progress at each of the plantations as well as any family or topical news. Somehow she found time to teach reading and music to her young sister as well as to some of the slave children. And she diligently maintained a daily journal in which she recorded her accomplishments and made an effort to learn from her mistakes. Eliza was rarely idle. Even her mother, who had disapproved of her daughter taking on the work of a man, had to accept that Eliza was assuming the role of plantation manager with a maturity beyond her years. Eliza would soon demonstrate her intelligence and vision for the future.

One example of her astuteness became apparent early on. Realizing she needed the support of her slave labor force, she built a nursery for their children and an infirmary for those who were injured or too sick to work. She also provided an adequate diet for the slaves and gained a general respect among them for her efforts—perhaps this young lady plantation mistress could carry on without Master Lucas's presence after all. Like the other Lowcountry planters, she began to explore the idea of other profitable export crops such as olives, grapes, nuts, hemp, and flax. Anything was possible in the young colony with a rich soil, temperate climate, and large labor force; the lure of new agricultural opportunities for wealth was rampant. George Lucas often corresponded with Eliza about testing some of these crops, and one day he sent her a package of seed that was to lead to her place in history.

Enclosed with the seed was a letter in which Lucas described a plant called indigo that had done well in Jamaica, and he was anxious for her to try it on their plantations. Indigo was a stalky plant whose leaves and stems, when carefully processed, produced a deep-blue vegetable dye. This dye was used in England in large quantities for coloring the Royal Navy's woolen uniforms as well as other textiles. No one had had any success growing indigo in the Province of South Carolina despite the temptation of the ready-made demand for the product. Eliza's neighbor, Mr. Deveaux, as well as others, warned of late frost and caterpillar damage to the crop and the difficulties of extracting the dye. But Eliza was not dissuaded. She shared her father's high hopes that this would add to the diversity of crops on his plantations and might even become another important export for colonial South Carolina.

However, the details of planting, harvesting, and processing the crop were daunting. Even if the plants survived the frosts and insects for harvesting, the processing was an extremely messy, labor-intensive task. The stems and leaves had to be soaked for a long time in large vats of hot water mixed with lime and animal urine until the essence was released into the liquid. The odor was quite foul. Then the mixture was boiled until the remaining mud-like residue could be scraped off into broad, flat molds. After it dried, it was cut into cakes ready for shipping.

Eliza launched into a meticulous process of trial and error in her first attempt. Her entire first year's efforts were a failure. She wrote her father that perhaps she had harvested the plants too soon or the temperature in the vats was too warm—or too cool. "I make no doubt Indigo will prove a very valuable Commodity in time," she wrote, and she asked to try again the following year to see if sowing the seeds earlier would make a difference. Her efforts the next year yielded better, if meager, results. She planted earlier in the spring and as the tender plants matured, the slaves rose at dawn to check for caterpillars. Eventually they learned to let chickens roam in the fields to consume these leaf-devouring pests. By August she had enough leaves for a test crop to harvest and process. Somehow in the sweltering summer heat, the slaves managed to maintain the constant fires beneath the giant vats. When the strong juice was extracted from the plant material, the color was a deep "navy blue." Eliza was elated even if her first crop had only resulted in six pounds of dye. She saw the potential and wrote her father, "We please ourselves with the prospect of exporting in a few years a good quantity from home and supplying the Mother Country with a manufacture for which she is now supplied from the French Colony . . . " The year was 1741 and Eliza was still only nineteen.

The news quickly spread, and Eliza gave away small quantities of indigo seeds to many area planters to encourage their cultivation and export of an ever-increasing amount to meet the strong British demand for the product. In fact, England was willing to pay a bounty for indigo grown in its own colony, and by 1749 they guaranteed a subsidy of sixpence per pound for the dried blocks of dyestuff. When the French and Indian War (1756–1763) made it even more difficult for English textile manufacturers to acquire the dark-blue dye from the French colonies in the West Indies, a boom market for the South Carolina product was created. At the peak, Lowcountry planters, and now many inland farmers, produced and shipped a million pounds of dye to Mother England, and large fortunes were made from the cultivation of indigo. For a time the staple crop was second only to rice, or "Carolina gold," as it was then called. Indigo continued to rank among the top exports until the American Revolution led to the cancellation of the bounty and a major disruption of the plantation economy.

Soon after Eliza's success with indigo, her neighbor and friend Col. Charles Pinckney became a widower. Eliza had visited often in the Pinckney's home providing good company to both the frail Mrs. Pinckney and Colonel Pinckney, often engaging them in lively conversation. Eliza was especially interested in books, and Colonel Pinckney delighted in loaning many to her from his extensive library, as well as discussing their various agricultural pursuits. After Mrs. Pinckney's death, Eliza married Charles Pinckney, who was nearly twice her age, on May 27, 1744. Colonel Pinckney, who was also an attorney and member of the Royal Council, was one of the wealthiest and most distinguished men of the Province. Upon their marriage Colonel Pinckney assumed the responsibilities of the Lucas plantations, and the couple settled into his Belmont Plantation five miles up the Cooper River from Charlestown. As a wedding gift for Eliza he also built a grand mansion in the city overlooking the bay. Together they continued to experiment with new, potentially profitable export crops. With some success Eliza planted mulberry trees to feed silkworms for the production of silk. They introduced other tropical fruit trees and plants, many sent to them by Eliza's mother and sister, Polly, who had rejoined her father on Antigua.

Colonel Pinckney, childless from his first marriage, had three children with Eliza, two sons and a daughter, each of whom garnered Eliza an additional note in South Carolina history as a very important matriarch. In 1753, Colonel Pinckney was appointed to represent South Carolina at the Board of Trade in London, and the family relocated there and enrolled the boys in British schools for a proper education. By May 1758 they returned to Charlestown to check on their properties, leaving their two sons in England to continue their schooling. While home, Colonel Pinckney succumbed to one of Charlestown's numerous malaria epidemics, dying that following July. Once more Eliza found herself thrust into the role of directing multiple plantations, family members, and slaves. Somehow she managed to adjust to her circumstances and prod her sons from afar to pursue success and honor in their learning, morals, and judgment. Again her persuasive letter writing skills were tested as she encouraged "self-control" and "reason over passion," attempting to mold their character. Unable to reunite with them for more than a decade, evidently Eliza's influence was strong and was a factor in their successful completion of their education at Westminster and Oxford, legal studies at the Middle Temple, and military training in France. She proudly declared, "well was she rewarded for the sacrifices she had made for their advantages, for her every wish was a command to her sons."

Yet in one very significant way, Charles Cotesworth and Thomas did defy their mother. As the events leading up to the

American Revolution unfolded, despite being raised to consider themselves British as both of their parents were before them, the sons rebelled by declaring their allegiance as "altogether American." In this regard they risked their lives and their family fortunes by serving as officers in the Revolutionary Army. Even daughter Harriott, after her marriage to wealthy rice planter and patriot Daniel Horry, risked her own personal safety by aiding patriot General Francis Marion in his stealth attacks on the British surrounding their home at Hampton Plantation. During the war Eliza sought refuge with her daughter at Hampton, located on the south Santee River forty miles north of Charlestown, and came to support the independence cause, enduring many hardships as a result. Toward the end of the British occupation of Charlestown, she despaired, "I have been robbed and deserted by my slaves; my property pulled to pieces, burnt and destroyed; my money of no value, my children sick and (taken) prisoners."

After the American victory, the family was able eventually to regain some of its property, and both sons distinguished themselves in the establishment of the new nation. Charles Cotesworth Pinckney was elected to the General Assembly in 1782. As one of South Carolina's most distinguished attorneys, he became a state delegate to the national Constitutional Convention in 1787. He served as U.S. minister to France (1796–1797). He was the Federalist Party candidate for vice-president in 1800, and ran for president in 1804 and again in 1808. Thomas Pinckney served as South Carolina governor (1787–1789) and presided at the State Convention, which ratified the U.S. Constitution. He was appointed U.S. minister to Great Britain (1791–1794) and negotiated the favorable Pinckney Treaty with Spain garnering additional American lands in the Southwest and free navigation of the Mississippi River. Thomas was the Federalist vice-presidential party candidate in 1796 and served as U.S. congressman (1797–1801).

To pay tribute to the mother of two such outstanding sons, President George Washington, on his southern tour of the young nation in 1791, made a special breakfast stop at Hampton Plantation, where the then elderly Eliza was living with her daughter, Harriott Horry. Two years later family lore maintains that, upon Eliza's death in Philadelphia where she had gone to seek cancer treatment, Washington once again paid homage by requesting to serve as a pall bearer at her funeral.

ANN PAMELA CUNNINGHAM

1846–1875

Preservationist

IT WAS A CLEAR, MOONLIT EVENING IN 1853 as the Potomac River steamer approached the Virginia plantation home and burial place of President George Washington widely known as Mount Vernon. As the steamboat passed by the famous landmark, it tolled its bell in respect—a custom still observed by all river craft some forty years after the president's death. One passenger, Mrs. Louisa Bird Cunningham, looked up from the deck railing toward the old mansion sitting high on the bluff. Mount Vernon stood there bathed in summer moonlight. What met Mrs. Cunningham's eyes was a shock to the South Carolina matron who held fond memories of visiting the home as a child. The roof sagged, the walls were pocked with peeling paint, and several of the huge, stately columns supporting the famous portico were missing, replaced by temporary supports from a half-dozen old ships' masts. The grounds were equally neglected with the walks and drives badly overgrown, the garden fences rotted away. Could this be the home of our nation's first president? How could it have come to this state of disrepair? Surely something must be done to protect this national treasure.

Overcoming poor health and many other obstacles, Pamela Cunningham led the efforts to preserve Mount Vernon for future generations.

Immediately, Mrs. Cunningham wrote to her daughter Pamela, back home at Rosemont, the family plantation in Laurens County, South Carolina. Her words conveyed her dismay:

> I was painfully depressed at the ruin and desolation of the home of Washington, and the thought passed through my mind: Why was it that the women of his country did not try to keep it in repair, if the men could not do it? It does seem such a blot on our country!

Her thoughts struck a chord with her thirty-seven-year-old semi-invalid daughter, who up until that time had long been searching for a meaningful purpose for her life. Pamela held her mother's letter to her chest and said to herself in bold defiance of her physical limitations, "I will do it."

Ann Pamela Cunningham was born on August 15, 1816, to Captain and Mrs. Robert Cunningham, prominent and wealthy landowners in upstate South Carolina. Robert Cunningham had inherited Rosemont from his father, Patrick, who had emigrated from Virginia around 1769. Captain Cunningham had enlarged the original house at Rosemont and, with great assistance from his wife, Louisa Bird, created what was considered one of the most beautiful and elaborate plantations in the Upcountry. Furnishings in the two-story mansion included many fine items imported from Europe such as a cut-glass French chandelier, an impressive book collection, hand-carved mahogany and rosewood furniture, and Wedgwood china, all of which reflected the prosperity of the couple. Mrs. Cunningham had also developed seven acres of flower gardens surrounding the house as well as a thirty-acre park beyond, in the midst of the large, self-sustaining, working farm. She collected plant specimens from around the world with some even coming from Mount Vernon, presented to her by Judge

Bushrod Washington, a George Washington descendant and old family friend.

Here on Rosemont, their only daughter, Pamela, led a privileged, sheltered life. She received an excellent education. At first, her schooling was handled by a governess and later she was a student at Barhamville, a leading academy for young women in Columbia, South Carolina. Pamela and her brother, John, were raised in a loving, happy, and devoutly religious atmosphere. The family worshipped together with their servants at Liberty Springs Presbyterian Church near the plantation. Befitting their social status, the Cunninghams entertained often, hosting barbecues, teas, dinner parties, and formal balls. Many of these occasions were attended by dignitaries from both the United States and abroad. This pampered, aristocratic life fostered self-confidence and a strong will in the young girl who was said to have remained unspoiled.

The pretty, auburn-haired seventeen-year-old must have held big dreams for her future. An accomplished horsewoman, Pamela regularly enjoyed riding the grounds of Rosemont with grace and ease. One day, however, she was thrown from her mount and suffered a severe spinal injury. She never fully recovered from the fall and, in fact, her condition gradually worsened over the years, confining her to a largely immobile life. Although she was not paralyzed, she must have had many long days of pain, depression, and sadness. Eventually, she drew upon her inner strength to turn her focus away from her physical problems and toward the welfare of her community, state, and country. Inspired by her mother's beseeching words, Pamela seized the opportunity to concentrate on righting the wrong she perceived as the neglected home of her nation's first president.

When friends and family learned of her plans, they tried to discourage her, concerned for her health. How could this petite woman who seldom left her parlor couch take on the task of raising a large sum of money to purchase and restore a run-down estate all the way up in northern Virginia? But Pamela Cunningham was determined.

Her initial appeal to the "Ladies of the South" appeared in the Charleston *Mercury* on December 2, 1853. Her letter pleaded: "Can you be still with closed souls and purses, while the world cries 'Shame upon America,' and suffer Mount Vernon, with all its sacred association, to become, as is spoken of and probably, the seat of manufacturers and manufactories? . . . Never! Forbid it . . . !" It was signed "A Southern Matron" in deference to the fact that the times dictated a proper lady's name should never appear in the newspaper other than announcing her marriage or her death. Modesty aside, the letter received immediate reaction and was picked up by many newspapers across the South.

The "Southern Matron" suggested that contributions should be sent to the governor of the donor's respective state, and in turn, each governor should forward all monies collected to the governor of Virginia, who would execute the purchase of the property. But these men had not been previously consulted and were not behind the cause. Undaunted, Miss Cunningham organized the Mount Vernon Ladies' Association, to receive contributions directly. Its goal was to raise the staggering $200,000 necessary to purchase the mansion and the surrounding two hundred acres that also included the site of Washington's tomb. Her plan was that then the Association would give the funds to the state of Virginia to purchase and hold title to Mount Vernon, offering it as a public resort overseen by the Ladies' Association.

But things did not go smoothly. The current owner, John Augustine Washington, a great-grand nephew of George Washington, was uncooperative. He was financially unable to maintain the property, due somewhat to the fact that many visitors from all over the world openly took advantage of Mr. Washington's hospitality. The sheer number of those visitors "paying their respect for its national significance" was driving Mount Vernon's owner toward bankruptcy. In desperation, Mr. Washington had previously offered Mount Vernon to the U.S. government and then the state of Virginia for the price of $100,000, and both had turned him down. He still wanted Virginia to own it but felt that they should pay for it out of state funds, not funds generated by a rather embarrassing fund-raising campaign publicizing its neglect. Nor was he confident that a group of women could raise such a large sum and continue its ongoing upkeep.

Another stumbling block came in the form of criticism from the Northern press contending that the fund-raising should be undertaken on a national scale. Miss Cunningham responded to this by appointing vice-regents for every state in the union, not just the Southern states, requiring each of them to form their individual committees and raise funds. With herself in place as regent, Pamela carefully selected women as vice-regents who were not only wealthy but also dedicated and influential in their respective areas of the country. The group then took on the new name of the Mount Vernon Ladies' Association of the Union, creating what was, in fact, America's first national preservation organization.

The fund-raising campaign started out slowly but caught on in Philadelphia during 1855 where clubs were formed and boxes for collecting contributions were placed in Independence Hall. School children were asked to respond to the call to preserve Washington's home by each giving a dime. But then another setback came when the notable men of Philadelphia decided to refuse their support stating that "they disapproved of women mixing in public affairs." This chauvinistic and discouraging attitude was prevalent for the time, but the ladies, inspired by their tireless leader, forged ahead.

In March 1856, enduring the long trip to Richmond, Virginia, Miss Cunningham attended the George Washington lecture delivered by the Reverend Dr. Edward Everett, considered the greatest orator of his generation. Dr. Everett had had a very impressive career as well—member of Congress, governor of Massachusetts, United States senator, minister to Great Britain, and president of Harvard University. After proper introductions Pamela so eloquently pleaded her case for his assistance in the Ladies' fund-raising efforts that he pledged to give all funds generated from his Washington orations around the country to their cause. This commitment raised more than $70,000 and attracted widespread attention to the movement. South Carolinians were so impressed by this gesture that, despite the fact that they were opposed to Dr. Everett's political views, he was granted free passage on all the state's railroads.

Just as things were looking up, more troubles developed when John Augustine Washington declined to accept the terms of the charter presented to him by the state of Virginia. When he refused to sell, contributions ceased and the press spread public distrust of the legitimacy of the Association. Again Miss Cunningham confronted the challenge by traveling to see Mr. Washington in person. She described her arduous journey, "I had not for many years been on a railroad—the motion made me ill. But I found I could get to Baltimore by canal boat, from whence the railroad ride would be short. Arrived at Mount Vernon, I was carried in a chair to the house on an awfully hot day in June. I saw the family; was received kindly; but all my arguments failed."

Disheartened Pamela departed, later writing:

When I got back to the wharf the boat had gone and left me! . . . I was put into a sailboat and towed into the stream, expecting to catch the mail boat, but waited in vain. When I got back to the bank I was nearly dead. But the moment I saw I was left I . . . said, "Mount Vernon is saved!" I was carried down to the parlor that night.

This twist of fate allowed Miss Cunningham to have more time with the Washingtons to relate the activities and accomplishments of the Association and their patriotic intent. Gradually the family and, most importantly, Mr. Washington were swayed by her ardent arguments, and as she was leaving the next morning, he agreed to resolve his objections, clearing the way for the purchase.

> I held out my hand—he put his in mine, then with quivering
> lips, moist eyes and a heart too full to speak, our compact was
> closed in silence. . . . None but God can know the mental labor
> and physical suffering Mount Vernon has cost me!

The new terms of the charter required that Virginia advance the $200,000, with the Ladies' Association reimbursing the state. Now Miss Cunningham was in the position of gaining the confidence of the state legislature that the Association would truly be able to repay the state the full amount, despite waning public interest and a national monetary panic during 1857. Returning to South Carolina on an airbed from Philadelphia where she often went for medical treatment, Pamela launched a new initiative in Charleston. With the support of the city's leading citizens, they named the Fourth of July as a day of public contributions to Mount Vernon. This fund-raiser helped spur renewed efforts around the country.

Another prominent figure of the day also came into play when Pamela enlisted the help of the well-known and highly respected Charleston lawyer, James L. Petigru. He drew up an effective constitution required by the charter for the organization, adding further legitimacy to their cause. With the charter and constitution in place, Miss Cunningham traveled back to Richmond in the hopes of getting the bill passed by the Virginia legislature. She wrote of these political struggles:

I was in desperate health, but to Richmond I had to go. There were doubts whether I should live to get there. We lost our bill, but I had a stronghold in the heart of John A. Washington. When this defeat came . . . he came to tell me we should have the title. We soon entered another bill, and carried it by acclimation, March 19, 1858.

The years of work had taken a toll on Pamela's health, and on the day of the signing of the purchase papers, she suffered a series of convulsions and was struggling for breath. Her friends were afraid she would not live to see the completion of her goal. With two vice-regents and lawyers present, after a while she rallied enough to sign her name a few letters at a time. Finally, the papers were signed, the sale was complete, and the documents were taken to the Virginia state archives.

Pamela recovered, and by 1859 the Mount Vernon Ladies' Association of the Union had liquidated most of the debt incurred at the purchase; they took possession of the property by 1860. The Association then turned its attention to raising funds for repairs and began restoration work with the threat of regional divisiveness looming. Pamela was undergoing further treatment in Philadelphia with plans to move to Mount Vernon to oversee the work in December 1860. But Pamela's father had died in 1859, and Pamela assumed the responsibilities of Rosemont for her elderly mother. Pamela left Mount Vernon in the care of her secretary, Sarah C. Tracy of New York, and the resident superintendent, Upton H. Herbert of Virginia, hoping to return there herself soon. The Civil War broke out the following year, and for six long years Pamela remained at Rosemont while war raged around her. Still, she didn't give up the campaign.

Often confined to her bed at Rosemont, Pamela dictated detailed instructions to Miss Tracy by letter, effectively directing all the affairs of Mount Vernon. Many times these letters were intercepted and censored, but she never gave up, nor did her able staff who withstood numerous trials while caring for the estate during the difficult war years. Somehow she was able to exact a pledge from both the Northern and Southern armies to respect the sacred ground of Washington's home—and, although the building was often within earshot of the guns, it remained untouched throughout the devastating conflict.

Once the war ended, the vice-regents and Miss Cunningham reunited at Mount Vernon and again took up the task of raising funds for the restoration. They decided to pursue obtaining an indemnity from the U.S. government for their use of the Association's boat, which had been impressed as a troop transport during the war and thus had denied the Association a chief source of revenue. Pamela went to the nation's Capitol and, employing her powers of persuasion, albeit while reclining on a sofa at times experiencing chills and a high fever, succeeded in seeing a bill passed that gave "$7,000 to be used in repairing the desolation at Mount Vernon."

From 1868 to 1872 she resided at Mount Vernon supervising the work directly since funds were so limited that a paid caretaker was no longer possible. Under her leadership, the Association's restoration progressed, refurnishing the mansion as closely as possible to its appearance in Washington's day.

By 1874 feeling that her work was done, Pamela Cunningham resigned as regent at the Association's annual meeting, delivering a farewell address:

> Ladies, the home of Washington is in your charge. See to it that you keep it the home of Washington. Let no irreverent hand change it; no vandal hands desecrate it with the fingers of progress! Those who go to the home in which he lived and died wish to see in what he lived and died!
>
> Let one spot in this grand country of ours be saved from change. . . . When thousands come from the ends of the earth,

let them see that, though we slay our forests, remove our dead, pull down our churches, remove from home to home till the hearthstone seems to have no resting place in America, let them see that we do know how to care for the Home of the Father of Our Country!

Miss Cunningham returned to Rosemont, where she intended to write the history of the Mount Vernon Ladies' Association and gain some much needed rest in the quiet surroundings of friends and family. She died there on May 1, 1875, within a year of her homecoming. A testament to her steadfast courage and sacrifice is the preservation of Mount Vernon for posterity. A tribute to her patriotism is her portrait in the South Carolina State House—the first painting of a woman displayed there.

MATILDA ARABELLE EVANS

1872-1935

Physician

FINALLY THE SUN WAS SETTING, AND MATILDA would soon be coming in from the fields to help her mother prepare supper for the family. She was tired from her long, hot day picking cotton in the dusty fields, bending over and over to pluck the fluffy fiber from its prickly bolls and stems. At least the repetitive work gradually filling her burlap sack gave her time to think about things, and twelve-year-old Matilda already had big dreams for her future. Her parents, born into slavery, had not had the chance for an education but told her often that education was the way out of the fields. She loved learning and had done well in school so far, and now was hoping to go to Aiken's innovative Schofield School. If she could just get in, she promised herself, she would work hard at her studies and not only have a better life but somehow strive to help others, too.

Matilda Evans was born to Anderson Evans and Harriett Corley on May 13, 1872, in Aiken County, South Carolina. She was the eldest of three children and grew up in the turbulent time of post-Reconstruction in the South, where racial violence and white separatism were the norm. Economic suppression and

Dr. Matilda A. Evans dedicated her life to improved
health care for her race.

disenfranchisement of blacks had taken hold, and opportunity for higher education and careers were scarce, especially for black women. Matilda's family was poor, but she remained focused on her goal to get an education. Her hard work paid off when she attracted the attention of Martha Schofield, a Quaker from Philadelphia who had founded The Schofield Normal and Industrial School in Aiken, one of the first Negro high schools in the country. Matilda was admitted to the school and, like the other students, worked in its gardens and cotton fields in addition to her studies.

Embracing this opportunity and Schofield's school motto of "thoroughness," Matilda impressed Martha Schofield with her diligence at all her tasks as well as her bright intelligence. Likewise, Schofield's strong values and courage in the face of adversity impressed Matilda. Schofield had founded the school in 1868 with financial assistance from Northern backers, braving "the threat of personal violence" while making "personal sacrifices" to educate blacks. Matilda Evans later wrote a biography of her mentor entitled *Martha Schofield, Pioneer Negro Educator,* as a tribute to Schofield's profound influence on her life. In the book Matilda stated that she would never forget Schofield "who had the heroic courage . . . to risk her life in the unselfish and holy cause of implanting in the Negro mind and soul that which is beautiful, noble and sentimental." She praised the School, which:

> has sent out into the world many young men and women who have gone back among their own people accomplished teachers, ministers, physicians, farmers and artisans. . . . No doubt the success which attended the efforts of the graduates of this School is due, in the main, to the strict regard for efficiency with which this great woman inspired every student coming under her influence.

Martha Schofield encouraged Matilda to pursue more education after graduation from the Schofield School and helped her attain funds to go to Oberlin College in Ohio. She studied there from 1897 to 1891, waiting tables to help work her way through school. From Oberlin she returned to the South to accept a one-year teaching position at Haines Institute in Augusta, Georgia. The following year she went back to Aiken to teach at Schofield Industrial School, saving money to pursue further education. Matilda had developed an interest in studying medicine in order to follow a dream of becoming a medical missionary in Africa. Schofield aided Matilda again by helping her gain admission to Women's Medical College in Philadelphia with financial assistance from a white benefactor named Alfred Jones. She was the only African-American student in her class and, after applying her "thoroughness" and strong work ethic, she received her medical degree there in 1897. By this time Matilda had had a change of heart about leaving the country to work as a missionary; she realized that her own South Carolina was sadly lacking in adequate health care for African Americans. Dr. Matilda Evans settled in Columbia, where she became the first native black female physician to work in South Carolina. (Non-native Dr. Lucy Hughes Brown, also a Women's Medical College graduate, was the first black female doctor, setting up practice in Charleston a few months prior to Evans.) There were only a handful of black male doctors in the state out of an overwhelmingly male-dominated profession.

Initially, Matilda treated both black and white patients in her home and also made house calls traveling by bicycle or horse and buggy. She was in great demand for her services in gynecology, obstetrics, and surgery.

Soon after setting up her practice, Dr. Evans witnessed first-hand the high mortality rate and general neglect of southern blacks. She strove to improve sanitation and accessible health care for her race and realized that the most serious need was for black hospitals. At the turn of the century, Columbia was a city of 25,000 with a black population of more than 40 percent, who were denied access to the city's hospital. Confident in her abilities, Evans set about in her efficient way to tackle the obstacles. In 1901 she gave up her successful private practice to found the Taylor Lane Hospital and Training School for Nurses and serve as its superintendent. She rented a one-story wooden-frame building with room for thirty patients. It was the first black hospital in Columbia and offered free health care and health education. A range of specialists, including a dentist, were on staff and offered a level of care rarely available to black people. Evans sometimes brought patients to the facility in her own wagon when they had no other transportation available. Patients came from as far away as Georgia and North Carolina seeking treatment that was unavailable to blacks in their home states.

By Taylor Lane's third year of operation, five hundred patients were treated in the wards, growing to six hundred the following year. To meet the financial challenges of running the hospital, Evans drew upon several sources of support. She made personal sacrifices by giving up her private practice to supervise and provide medical services at the hospital. Student nurses contributed their labor in exchange for the training and housing. They also were "hired out" to provide nursing services for pay, which they dutifully turned over to the hospital. More support came from young white physicians who volunteered their time to gain clinical experience. Evans courted them by praising their contribution of "time and assistance at any hour, night or day . . . to do the work of this Hospital free of charge." Using all her considerable persuasive talents, Evans developed collaborative relationships between Taylor Lane and companies employing large numbers of black workers. She negotiated with the white owners/managers of the Southern, Seaboard Line, and Atlantic Coast Line railroad companies, the

Columbia Light and Power Company, and many major factories. She set up contracts to care for their employees at a fee of one dollar a day. Later, the hospital building was destroyed by fire, but Evans started another hospital that moved to a larger facility, named St. Luke's Hospital and Training School for Nurses, which operated until 1918.

In 1907, when writing to Alfred Jones on behalf of another promising young African-American student wanting to attend the Women's Medical College, Matilda recounted:

> You may remember me as being the colored student to whom you gave a scholarship in 1893 to The Woman's Medical College of Penn. I graduated in the class of 1897 and came South and have built up, as I must tell you, a most enviable reputation. I have done well, and have a very large practice among all classes of people. . . . I have had unlimited success . . . Since I have returned to my native state, others have been inspired and have gone to our beloved College to take degrees.

Many wealthy white women also sought her care, perhaps because they preferred a female doctor or appreciated her discretion in caring for their medical problems away from the members of their own social class. Their patronage supplied the majority of Dr. Evans's income and allowed her to treat black women and children free of charge. It also gave her a degree of acceptance and recognition among white people in her community. Her charitable work among her own race garnered their respect for her ability and authority. In a laudatory article in *The State,* Columbia's leading newspaper, the headline proclaimed Evans "South Carolina's Brainiest Negro" and "a Black Woman, Who has Saved Hundreds of Lives and Has Educated Many Trained Nurses." Testimonials from her white male colleagues praised "her devotion to her work and her earnest Christian character" and stated that the nurses in her training school were "sought after by the doctors and the better class of people of our city." *The Palmetto Leader,* a black newspaper, asserted that "The State of South Carolina has not produced, within our group, a citizen more meritoriously outstanding" and that her spirit of altruism was a "consuming zeal to render service rather than to accumulate money or to acquire popularity." Evans's unprecedented ability to gain this respected status across the segregated boundaries in turn-of-the-century South Carolina laid the foundation for her advocacy for progressive social reform.

Evans started the Negro Health Care Association of South Carolina to convince more people that individuals following proven health practices and safe sanitary habits could improve their own health. She founded a weekly newspaper, *The Negro Health Journal of South Carolina,* in 1916 to help spread the message of preventative medicine and other health-related issues. She repeatedly argued that the sick Negro not only endangered his or her white employer but also the larger community as well. One article headline read "Cheap Living, Poverty, Disease and Death Lay Heavy Annual Tax on People Everywhere." She felt that the low wages paid to blacks prevented their ability to be clean and healthy. "Cheap [domestic] help contaminate your home even the very food you eat because they can not be clean, healthy and honest on the wages they get." In addition to her appeals for adequate pay, she sought funds to support a visiting-nurse health program. Adding her voice to the refrain that germs knew no skin-color distinction, she held that whatever illness beset the black worker would sooner or later make its way into white households. At a time of widespread tuberculosis epidemics, she felt that visiting nurses could help prevent the spread of the highly communicable disease. In addition to the loss of life, she told her readers, black illness and death robbed South Carolina of some $20 million in economic impact every year.

But the white separatist voices grew louder still. In South Carolina, as well as across the region, they appealed to whites to support policies that prevented racial contact, fostering a separation of the races wherever possible. Local and state governments largely ignored black entreaties for improved infrastructure for fresh water, sewer systems, and paved streets as well as clinics and sanitariums. The problem grew worse, as reflected in the disproportionately high infant mortality and tuberculosis death rates among blacks in southern communities. Evans's work became more focused on community activism designed to counteract the entrenchment of these attitudes in Columbia and throughout South Carolina. She was committed to increasing pressure on the state to take responsibility for the health care of its black citizens.

She was especially concerned about black children who often went without checkups or vaccinations. She approached Columbia public school authorities to grant her permission to examine the children. She personally paid for many physical examinations and immunizations for black students. Her survey in the schools found numerous ailments and diseases afflicting the children. As a result of her findings, the school district agreed to set up a permanent physical examination program within the public school system. Next, Evans began calling upon black religious leaders, black businessmen, and black club women to unite their efforts behind a free clinic for African-American children and expectant mothers. She held meetings in her home organizing three clubs—one for men, another for women, and one for girls—so that each group could go from church to church and school to school gaining support for the clinic. With this coalition of support, the State Board of Health was forced to acknowledge the black community's resolve and needs. They promised vaccines, and the Richland County legislative delegation made an appropriation of five hundred dollars to establish a temporary free clinic housed in the basement of the Zion Baptist Church.

As the country plunged into the Great Depression, Dr. Evans never wavered. In July 1930 the clinic opened to a long line of children and parents waiting to receive free vaccinations. In fact *The Palmetto Leader* reported that seven hundred came in for free services on the first day. By September the newspaper stated that 3,187 had been examined and 1,108 vaccinated and that a "steady stream of hundreds continues each day to come." Evans did not let up, giving lectures and interviews to the media to keep up the pressure on state and county leaders. She pronounced "I am determined—I have sworn it—that . . . our children shall not be deprived of the advantages which a first class, most modern clinic can give."

The demand for the clinic's services were so great that it soon became a permanent operation, and both the State Board of Health and the Richland County legislative delegation continued to allocate funds from their budgets to maintain it, until Evans's death in 1935. Fortunately, the passage of the Social Security Act the same year provided a public maternal and child health program that carried on the work begun by Dr. Evans. Perhaps just as importantly, the Columbia Clinic success taught Columbia's black citizens a valuable lesson in the power of mobilization to achieve their goals. Evans helped others to realize that applying pressure on the state to make changes would lead to greater access of opportunity for blacks. The severe economic hardships of the Depression also fostered black rejection of "separate but equal" when black professionals realized that they could not sustain separate health care facilities (and other institutions) in this time of economic collapse. Following Evans's lead, they would need to unite and mobilize to demand their rights of citizenship in a desegregated society in the years ahead.

Somehow Evans found time for other pursuits in the midst of a demanding, trailblazing career. On her own, she raised eleven children who were without a home, including some who had been left at her practice and five children of her late sister. She emphasized education, respect, cleanliness, and good manners and gave them all the opportunity to go to college. Evans owned a twenty-acre farm off Two Notch Road in northeast Columbia, where she raised chickens, cows, and pigeons and grew vegetables and fruit trees. She set up a recreational center there, offering a program for underprivileged boys ages eight to sixteen. She taught herself to swim and opened a pool where she taught the boys to swim as well. She also enjoyed dancing, knitting, and playing the piano. She was an active member of St. Luke's Episcopal Church, serving as an officer in the Episcopal Church, Upper Diocese of South Carolina.

Matilda Evans died on November 17, 1935, and is buried in Palmetto Cemetery in Columbia.

Dr. Evans's professional achievements are reflected in the recognition she received in her lifetime. In 1922 she was elected president of the all-black Palmetto State Medical Society, the first woman to hold this office in a time when hostility toward women in the medical profession was common, even among black physicians. She also served as vice president of the National Medical Association and was appointed to the Volunteer Medical Service Corps during World War I. She organized and served as president of the Colored Congaree Medical Society. She served as a trustee of Haines College in Augusta, Georgia. More recently, in tribute to her lifelong dedication to the service of others through the medical profession, Richland Memorial Hospital in Columbia named an award in her honor.

JULIA MOOD PETERKIN

1880–1961

Pulitzer Prize–Winning Author

JULIA WALKED BRISKLY TO HER FOREMAN'S CABIN wondering what she could possibly do to fix Frank Hart's feet, which had suddenly stopped supporting him. His wife, Charity, had tried everything she knew—hot poultices and a specially brewed tea of violet leaves and beargrass; she had even bought charms from the plantation medicine man to ward off the conjure. Nothing had worked. When she entered the cabin, Julia immediately caught the odor of meat cooking only to realize to her shock that Frank's foot was the source. Incredibly, he sat unflinching next to the fireplace with his foot on a hot coal. It was quite evident that he had no feeling in his feet, and she was unsure what to do next. As mistress of Lang Syne Plantation she must not show her fear or her lack of composure. She proceeded to bathe his feet in warm water to which she added a drop of disinfectant mainly hoping that her attention would encourage him and lift his spirits, and possibly somehow improve his circulation. As he sat with his feet in the soaking tub, soon she was horrified to see five toes bobbing on the surface.

Charity and Frank immediately blamed Julia's treatment for the loss of his toes, but in reality he was suffering from senile gangrene,

In this photographic portrait by her friend Doris Ullman, Pulitzer-prize winner Julia Peterkin strikes a reflective pose.

and his toes had rotted off as a result of the advanced stage of the disease. Julia summoned her father, Dr. Julius Mood, who eventually had to amputate the foreman's legs, only extending his life for a short time. Before he died, Frank had one request of Julia, "Bury me in a man-sized box. . . . I been six foot fo'."

The drama of these tragic events marked a turning point in Julia Peterkin's life as she grappled with lingering guilt over the event and personal doubt. Over the next weeks she would scrutinize her life and conclude that she was not living up to her full capabilities. The cycles of life on a farm from planting through harvesting and the passing of seasons as well as the births, arduous lives, and deaths of the five hundred or so former slaves still working on Lang Syne served as constant reminders of her own mortality.

Julia Mood was born on October 31, 1880, in Laurens County, South Carolina, the third daughter of Alma Archer and Julius Mood. Alma died of tuberculosis when Julia was just a toddler. Honoring Alma's dying request, Dr. Mood had sent young Julia to live with her paternal grandparents, while keeping her two older sisters with him. Her grandfather, Henry Mood, was a Methodist minister who instilled self-discipline, proper speech, good manners, and strong values in Julia at an early age. His ministerial duties led them from town to town, and Julia was always separated from her siblings in Sumter, South Carolina. Julia's father remarried and raised the two older girls and later their half-brother with his second wife, Janie. Julia despised her stepmother and didn't want to be anywhere near her, but she could never quite overcome the feeling that she had been cast aside because her father did not love her. She would strive for his attention and approval throughout his long life.

In May 1897 when Julia was sixteen years old, her grandfather died of congestive heart failure. She rejoined her family in Sumter, only to set off for college with her older sister, Laura, the following fall. They entered Columbia College in the state capital, where they were quite unhappy. In rebellion they created such mischief that they were sent home before the end of the year. Before they could unpack, Dr. Mood sent them off to a new school in Spartanburg, South Carolina, called Converse College. There, the girls settled in and attained their degrees. Julia stayed an additional year earning a Master of Arts before seeking a teaching position, against her father's wishes. She found a job at a one-room schoolhouse with fewer than ten pupils in rural Fort Motte, in the midlands of South Carolina.

This community of Fort Motte was home to the Peterkin family, one of the area's prominent families, who owned and farmed Lang Syne Plantation, a fifteen-hundred-acre pre-Revolutionary tract known for its productive and wisely managed land. Julia met the family when she boarded with Lizzie Peterkin while working at the school. Soon Julia, a tall, striking young woman with bright red hair, caught the attention of Lizzie's brother, Willie Peterkin, who was heir to the plantation. They were married in July 1903, and Julia began her life as a plantation mistress. It was a role for which she was totally unprepared. Even though she had servants to prepare meals and take care of her household, she was expected to tend to the needs of the four hundred to five hundred black people who lived on Lang Syne as sharecroppers. This encompassed everything in their daily lives ranging from farming to personal to medical problems. Feeling overwhelmed, she wasn't sure how to begin.

Soon motherhood became another dimension in Julia's new life. After a difficult delivery, William George Peterkin Jr. was brought into the world by his grandfather, Dr. Mood. Learning that she would not be able to have any additional children, Julia sank into a severe postpartum depression that lasted for two years. She refused to get out of bed until one day Lavinia Berry, nurse to Julia and baby Bill, accosted her. Lavinia was a former slave and had cared for Willie Peterkin as an infant. She explained that the "hands" were looking to Julia to assume the old, traditional role of plantation mistress to "dominize" and nurture them. She must get up out of the bed and get on with life; she was needed—plain and simple. Lavinia, or "Vinner," enticed her with stories of the goings-on in the Quarters, the old slave cabins of Lang Syne. She told gossip of people settling arguments with knives, seducing each other's mates, having illegitimate children, and generally leading bold and forthright, if emotional, lives. Julia was entranced with these lives surrounding her, so different from her own. Soon she learned much more about the daily work life of the Gullahs—ex-slaves or slave descendants. How they had an intimate knowledge of agriculture, animal husbandry, and the natural environment. She recognized that much of their know-how stemmed from sharp observation and passed-down wisdom interspersed with superstition. Julia developed an admiration for their skills and quickly began to absorb their ways.

At the same time she embraced the social life among her own peer group by attending teas, card parties, and other society gatherings. She actively participated in cultural organizations such as the Afternoon Music Club, the Daughters of the American Revolution, and the United Daughters of the Confederacy. Her other hobbies included cultivating roses and experimenting with horticulture. She raised Llewellyn setters, pigeons, and white Holland turkeys. She traveled to Europe and enjoyed the benefits of a life provided by her hardworking and capable husband. In addition to managing the large cotton plantation, Willie and his brother owned most of the commercial outlets in Fort Motte including a grocery store, bank, and pharmacy. Capitalizing on the growing market for cotton by-products, they ran a cotton gin and a cottonseed oil mill. Over time Willie shouldered the responsibilities of supporting a larger, extended family including his widowed sister and sisters-in-law and providing for the plantation workers who depended on him for food, clothing, and shelter. He dedicated his life to a pursuit of agricultural and entrepreneurial success with a practical, determined focus.

Julia and Willie's lives passed undisturbed in this conventional manner for many years until a series of misfortunes altered their course. Willie became ill, suffering a ruptured appendix, leaving him a semi-invalid and putting Julia in a much more responsible position of actually running the plantation. Some of their livestock contracted a fatal illness, and the foreman, Frank Hart, to whom Julia turned for help, had lost his legs and his desire to live. Her feelings of guilt over his fate and the other problems of Lang Syne led her to profess:

> It seemed to me that everything in the world had gone wrong, and I felt a sense of personal responsibility, as though I had got out of touch with the creative forces or had gone against the rules of the game, else I would have had the inner strength to meet these problems as they came.

She sought a creative outlet, perhaps as a complete change from her duties at Lang Syne, or as a way to pursue an abandoned dream of becoming a concert pianist. She decided to study music again and began piano lessons with Dr. Henry Bellaman, an instructor at Chicora College, forty miles away in Columbia. In relating the story of Frank Hart as her catalyst for self-examination and change, Dr. Bellaman, also a fiction writer as well as a music teacher, recognized her storytelling gift. He encouraged Julia to write down her experiences and bring a new sketch to each of their sessions. At first she resisted, saying she had no talent for writing, but the seed was planted and began to take hold.

One evening Bellaman brought his friend, the famous poet Carl Sandburg, to visit the Peterkins at Lang Syne. During the course of the visit, Sandburg asked to see some of Julia's sketches and suggested she submit them for publication. Concerned that his compliments were said out of politeness, she asked for the name of the toughest critic in the literary world who might render a completely impartial opinion of her work. Sandburg named H. L. Mencken in New York. Julia gathered her courage and sent samples for his review. Mencken was immediately interested and accepted one for his own magazine, *Smart Set*. He also recommended her work to Emily Clark, who was publishing a new magazine called *The Reviewer* in Richmond, Virginia. Miss Clark, who was interested in promoting Southern literature, published Julia's stories in more than a dozen issues of *The Reviewer*. This early success of what Julia called her "crude, really stark plantation sketches" allowed the new writer, now in her forties, to develop and gain confidence without the disappointment of severe editing and rejections. And as a result of this national exposure and her influential literary friends, Mrs. Peterkin was offered a contract by Alfred A. Knopf to write a book about her plantation blacks.

The result was a book called *Green Thursday,* a collection of twelve short stories about a black family—Killdee and Rose Pinesett, and their children, Jim, Sis, Missie, and little Rose—and their struggles with poverty and personal tragedy. The book was released in September 1924 and eventually sold more than five thousand copies, validating Mrs. Peterkin's talent.

As pleased as she was about its success, at the same time she began to worry about her Southern audience's reaction to her unsentimental portrayals of black people told from their own point of view. She realized that she now had a more widespread readership beyond the limited distribution of her previous magazine articles. Her fears were justified when local society as well as close friends and members of her own family criticized her and feared that she would bring social ostracism to them by association. It was felt that the socially prominent Mrs. Peterkin must maintain a certain decorum and tend to her responsibilities at home. To turn her back on these duties to write fiction was disgraceful, especially if she became the subject of news stories. Polite opinion in her day held that no lady's name should appear in the newspaper except for regarding her wedding or her death. And to compound the situation, her fiction's subject matter was highly controversial—arson, disfigurement, adultery, and death of blacks in graphic detail were not acceptable topics for a female author. Even her father, who prided himself on his open-minded worldliness, wished that she would write "more ladylike stories." Although stung, she handled the criticism with poise and focused on the "joy of having some real critics to encourage me to go on."

Sandburg wrote, "It's a real and fine book." Another respected voice, Joel Springarn, offered that "nothing so stark, taut, poignant, has come out of the white South in fifty years." Favorable reviews appeared in the *New York Times, Time Magazine, The Saturday Review of Literature,* the *Chicago Evening Post* and other leading publications around the country. Of special interest to Julia was the reaction of black leaders to her book. Here she found encouragement as well and she felt sanctioned by the words of W.E.B DuBois in *Crisis,* the official publication of the NAACP, when he wrote that "She (Mrs. Peterkin) is a Southern white woman but she has the eye and ear to see beauty and to know truth." In general they recognized that she was making an honest attempt to avoid the old, condescending stereotypes popular in 1920s America perpetuated by the Ku Klux Klan as well as the black-faced entertainers like Al Jolson, dubbed "the World's Greatest Entertainer."

Now she was beginning to consider the task of undertaking a full-blown novel, expanding her horizons beyond *Green Thursday*'s collection of stories. Her literary friends advised her to go slowly, advice that she took to heart. She remained true to her own experiences on Lang Syne Plantation. "When you are writing out of your experience you don't have to rely to any great extent upon your imagination. I have lived among the Negroes. They are my friends, and I have learned so much from them. The years on the plantation have given me plenty of material, my life has been rich, so why try to improve upon the truth?" Over the next three years, she wove the terrible story of her foreman, Frank Hart, into the book, *Black April*. She switched publishers from Knopf, which had expressed their view that the book would have limited sales potential, to Bobbs-Merrill, which launched the book with a major advertising campaign. The novel found both financial and critical success. The literary editor of the Nashville *Tennessean,* Donald Davidson, wrote a very favorable review of the book, representative of other enlightened southern critics' reviews. "It is powerful, serene, good-humored, tempestuous by turns, with all the primitive passions kept for so many years in their undisturbed original state . . . it is . . . the first genuine novel in English of the Negro as a human being." On a national level, *The Saturday Review of Literature* and *The New Republic* praised "Mrs. Peterkin's achievement" . . . "where other fiction of Negro life seems false." These accolades from contemporary northern critics, who generally held a hostile view of the South and its racial attitudes, gained her a place among the southern progressives of the 1920s and '30s. Even at home she began to receive local honors and acceptance as her celebrity grew.

She was invited to spend the summer of 1927 at the MacDowell Colony in Peterborough, New Hampshire, a writers' retreat conducive to creative thought and output. Here she began a new work of fiction telling the story of a black plantation woman, whom she had treated only briefly in an earlier *Reviewer* sketch. Her protagonist, Mary Pinesett, is independent and full of life and provides the perfect character to further portray plantation life. The story takes Mary from a young woman to middle age when she renounces her wayward life of numerous lovers and illegitimate children. She turns back to the church, but only after she has shamed her sanctimonious enemies while holding onto her good-hearted personality. The book, *Scarlet Sister Mary,* was completed in less than a year and published in 1928. The reviewers were even more enthusiastic than they had been about *Black April,* and it quickly became a best seller. Another factor contributing to its strong sales was the banning of the book in Boston, among several other works by leading authors of the day such as Theodore Dreiser, Upton Sinclair, and Bertrand Russell. The national publicity of this ban generated even more demand for these authors' books.

Talk began circulating that *Scarlet Sister Mary* should be considered for the Pulitzer Prize for Fiction. Although Mrs. Peterkin was doubtful that it would win, on May 14, 1929, the announcement was made that it had indeed won. That day the publisher kept five presses busy printing additional copies, anticipating the demand. It was printed in Spanish as well and was the first American literary novel to appear in a paperback form. All editions eventually sold over a million copies and made Julia Peterkin a national celebrity.

Enjoying her latest success, Mrs. Peterkin was sought out to write articles by the high-paying, mass circulation magazines such as *The Saturday Evening Post* and *Ladies' Home Journal.* Over the next few years she wrote for these publications and worked on her last novel, *Bright Skin,* the story of Cricket, a mulatto girl who endures the ostracism of the plantation blacks during her childhood. Finally, searching for acceptance, she flees to New York and becomes part of Harlem's segregated community. *Bright Skin,* published in 1932, did not fare well among the critics who felt that it neither covered new ground nor improved upon familiar insights. The book may also have been a victim of the changing times and the new appetite for antiestablishment works about social protest as the country plunged into the Depression.

Although Mrs. Peterkin was discouraged by this poor reception of her latest book, she decided to tackle a work of nonfiction with her good friend Doris Ullman. Ullman was a successful photographer who was known for her portraits of the famous as well as the oppressed. Their collaboration produced *Roll, Jordan, Roll,* which paired Ullman's brooding, powerful portraits of the plantation Gullahs with Peterkin's short essays and vignettes about their lives. Her topics covered the cycle of plantation life including the institution of slavery and its hardships, complex family relationships, religious beliefs, traditions, folklore, and superstitions. Published in 1933, the book met their goal of capturing the plantation culture before it disappeared from America's memory, and it is considered an important documentary of our nation's social history.

Roll, Jordan, Roll was Julia's final major work. After her husband's death in 1939, she returned her focus to the management of Lang Syne and to her family, which by then included a grandson, and to Democratic Party politics. But she continued to stay active in the literary world teaching, lecturing, and writing articles. After a short illness at the age of eighty, she died on August 10, 1961.

Overall, her place in American literature is still debated. The success of her novels had garnered her international fame, a fame unlike any seen up until that time. She had intrigued large numbers of white readers with her strange tales of black farm laborers who lived largely unknown lives based on African origins and plantation structure. Where many others had failed, she worked out a literary depiction of the Gullah language that captured the flavor of the dialect but was at the same time readable by the general public. She dealt with subjects considered not only racy but also politically hot in the South during the period of the Jim Crow laws. Her work as a whole is valuable as it records the declining plantation economy and the flight of the blacks leaving their familiar rural world behind and seeking greater opportunity in the cities of the North and entering mainstream society.

LAURA BRAGG

1884–1978

First Female Museum Director

UNFAMILIAR SIGHTS, SMELLS, AND SOUNDS bombarded the senses of twenty-eight-year-old Laura Bragg as she sailed into Charleston Harbor, anticipation of her new life in the South brewing within her. The Clyde Line steamer *Arapahoe* docked just after lunchtime on September 1, 1909. Even though it was still hot, there was a hint of autumn in the air, sunlight bounced off the grand mansions of the High Battery, and the crepe myrtle blossoms and palmetto tree fronds tossed lightly in the sea breeze. Laura could hardly wait to disembark and explore her new hometown that greeted her with a shabby but charming elegance. She stepped ashore to find streets that were mostly dirt with crushed oyster shells, brick, gravel, and cobblestones paving the roadways through the oldest sections of the city. The marsh grass and salt air barely masked the odors of the thousands of privies that were the primary sewer system for the town's residents. But she also discovered a town that had magnificent, if weathered, architecture that had withstood the Civil War, the great earthquake of 1886, and major hurricanes and fires in just her most recent history. Like its architecture, Charleston still

Miss Laura Bragg, shown here ca. the 1920s, led the Charleston Museum
into the twentieth century.

stood proud but was stuck in the aftermath of these disasters with an economic, social, and cultural stagnancy untouched by present-day modernization. To a New Woman in the Progressive Era these circumstances represented a challenge and an opportunity to make her mark, and Laura Bragg intended to do just that.

Laura's early life was spent in Massachusetts as the eldest child of a Methodist minister and his wife, the Reverend Lyman Bragg and Sarah Klotz Bragg. She was born on October 9, 1881, and was followed by a brother, Ernest, and sister, Barbara, which comprised their active, middle-class family. At the age of six Laura contracted scarlet fever, which resulted in hearing loss that grew progressively worse over the course of her life. Her father refused to acknowledge this as a handicap in his daughter and instead focused on immersing his bright, curious child in his world of learning and books. She was raised to take pride in her ancestry, which her father had traced all the way back to William LaGrande, grand porteur of William the Conqueror, through her colonial ancestors who had arrived in America as early as 1630. Perhaps with this proud lineage in mind, her parents took up reform-minded causes of their day such as the American Association of Colored Youth and the Women's Christian Temperance Union. Their involvement in civic and community projects set an example for their young daughter. Reverend Bragg's influence was especially strong in Laura's development. He had assembled a sizeable, personal library that covered a broad range of topics including theology, philosophy, literature, and science. Laura, who possessed a remarkable memory, absorbed much of this material and discussed her thoughts with "Dadda dearest," her teacher, confidant, and mentor. Reverend Bragg continued this close father/daughter relationship with his eager student through visits and correspondence throughout his life.

Laura's formal education in high school took place in Amesbury, Massachusetts, and Lisbon, New Hampshire, where her father served as minister in Methodist churches. She then attended Simmons College in Boston and was a member of its first graduating class in 1906. It was a good fit for her since she was immersed in the cultural opportunities offered in a cosmopolitan metropolis. The Boston Museum of Fine Arts and the Natural History Museum were two of her favorite haunts for soaking up art and botany. The college itself was founded on the intent of preparing its female students for an independent, professional career. At the time, only a handful of colleges were involved in training young women beyond traditional roles, and Laura Bragg had very different aspirations from those of most young women of her generation. She studied library science, which was a new course offering, since most libraries trained their own staff. Her course work included cataloging, handwriting, typing and shorthand, English, French, German, and physics; and later economics, biology, business methods, accounting, and library economy and practices. An additional curriculum requirement was to serve an apprenticeship each semester at a museum or library. One of these experiences placed her with Charles Johnson, curator of the Museum of the Boston Society of Natural History. Under his guidance she learned to conduct bird surveys and to press and preserve flowers and ferns while training in the hands-on work of the museum. All these college experiences engaged and intrigued Laura, who thirsted for more education and experience.

After receiving her Bachelor of Science degree in Library Science in June, Laura took a position as the librarian for a social service library on Orr's Island, just off Maine's coast. The island was largely a fishing community with generations of the same families eking out a living from the sea. She had very full days teaching and reading to the children and helping everyone find books. Her social work included teaching the adults basic everyday skills like how to give haircuts, cut out patterns to make clothing, and care for infants.

Her love of botany was fostered as she studied the flora and fauna and gathered specimens to mount. The children often brought her butterflies, flowers, and insects, and the fishermen brought her interesting sea creatures. She also was able to further her studies of biology and botany at Tufts College Biological Laboratory, which was located just across the bay. Although the position was to last only one year, she decided to stay longer perhaps due to a strong feeling that she was making a difference in the lives of the island-ers. But by 1908 the severe, long-lasting winter climate proved too much for her, and she left Orr's Island for a temporary position as a teacher's assistant at the New York City Public Library. She had also begun a correspondence with the director of South Carolina's Charleston Museum, Paul Rea. The Charleston Museum had the distinction of being the oldest museum in the western hemisphere, and Rea, with his plans to bring a new twentieth-century focus, enticed Laura Bragg to come to Charleston to work at the museum. As the museum's librarian and Rea's assistant, Bragg could partici-pate in this exciting transformation utilizing all her training and sat-isfying her social reform zeal in the provincial south while enjoying a much milder climate.

Reflecting the city's economically depressed state, The Charleston Museum was in dire need of funding to launch its new mission. Its existence up until that point was as a part of the College of Charleston, and the collection was housed in a classroom on its campus. Dr. Rea taught biology and pre-med classes at the College of Charleston and embryology and physiology at the Medical Col-lege nearby, while also serving as the curator of the museum. He successfully persuaded Charleston City Council to fund the muse-um's operations and purchase Thompson Auditorium, which con-tained 35,000 feet of floor space in the heart of the city at Rutledge Avenue and Calhoun Street. The purchase of and move to the new facility set in motion the teamwork between Rea and Bragg that began the new era for the museum. Bragg's direct responsibilities included installing and caring for the old museum's collection in Thompson Auditorium. Although funds for acquiring new books were limited, she directed the binding of hundreds of used books and periodicals, which led to ease of use by the public and the potential for circulation on a lending basis outside the museum. She was also in charge of the Department of Public Instruction, which primarily meant she directed the Natural History Society's efforts to provide lectures and demonstrations for classes all the way from kindergarten through college levels as well as for business groups. As its president she guided a project to survey the trees in the city, and the growing membership collected information on the numerous species and varieties.

In the summer of 1910 Laura Bragg returned home to visit her family in New Hampshire and to share her learning and enthusiasm for her new job with her father. She combined this trip with visits and work at the Boston Museum of Natural History, where she studied birds, mollusks, and trees. Beginning what would become a summer routine over the years, she visited many other Northern museums, as well, absorbing their educational exhibits. She realized that the successful institutions had moved away from the old purpose of serving as scientific repositories for inanimate objects toward becoming public institutions that were striving to engage and educate a broader audience through carefully planned and organized exhibits. She shared these ideas with Rea and brought them back to The Charleston Museum. Subsequently, her installations soon bore new, illustrated labels meant to inform and entertain visitors.

This shift in focus meant that The Charleston Museum would have to extend its reach in the community and find new patrons across all the social classes, even including its black citizens. While this concept was just emerging in the museums of the Northeast, it was still unheard of among the scattered museums in the isolated, racially divided, and poverty-stricken South. The social reformer in Bragg seized the concept that museums were potentially powerful institutions for self-improvement. Her work at The Charleston Museum gave her "an opportunity to do good for ordinary people on a massive scale."

One way to start was to interest young people at an early age. When the museum moved to its new location, she enlisted the help of the younger members of the Natural History Society to assist in carrying some of the collections of the local shells, bird nest and eggs, bones, and the smaller animal specimens. Her hopes of sparking an interest in learning and the museum were realized as many of these children and their families became lifelong friends and supporters of the museum. She began her outreach programs by teaching classes to schoolchildren who came to the museum for instruction and began giving monthly talks to the Association of First Grade Teachers on adapting nature lessons to the local environment. By the end of 1912, Bragg had compiled twelve ways of assisting both public and private schools in Charleston County in natural history programs. These included a lecture room and presenter, a guide to the museum's collections, copies of Bragg's Charleston Nature Study Course, field trips, and a reading room. (No free library existed in Charleston until 1931.)

She had also packaged twenty-five traveling school exhibits on a variety of subjects in portable wooden cases that could be carried into the classrooms. Some of these contained specimen animals like the southern fox squirrel or a lion cub, animal and plant life from the beach at nearby Isle of Palms, and an iron and steel exhibit. These caught on quickly in the public schools, and it was reported that year that they were used along with the Nature Study Course by 1,750 students in twenty-eight classes. These traveling exhibit cases came to be known as "Bragg Boxes" and grew greatly in popularity, exceeding even Bragg's expectations. They became a key tool in fulfilling her desire to expose large numbers of children both black and white to the natural world around them. They also stirred interest in visits to the museum and eventually were requested at schools around South Carolina as well as Massachusetts. Later educators in Richmond, Virginia; San Antonio, Texas; Rochester, New York; Kalamazoo, Michigan; and Wake County, North Carolina, asked for them for their schools too, gaining national recognition for Bragg and the museum.

In 1914 the Board of Public School Commissioners, impressed by the educational work of the museum, passed a special resolution further aligning the city schools with the institution. Primary-grade teachers were required to use Bragg's nature study course and bring their students to the museum for classes. Many of them also attended summer classes there on nature study, area geography, and local history taught by Bragg for course credit. Within the museum she tackled a "History of Man" exhibit to chronicle the "development of civilization from the most primitive peoples through the Egyptians and Assyrians to modern times." She employed large, imposing casts of Egyptian and Assyrian sculptures in the collection to immediately grab the viewer's attention. Then she combined them with other old exhibits, cleaning and displaying them to illustrate broadly the historical time line. This exhibit exemplified her intent to use the old exhibits in a new way "to conform to the fundamental theory that it is the use rather than the mere preservation of the material (that) is important." Bragg the librarian continued to work on the museum's book collection, soliciting volumes and donations from individuals both locally and beyond. By 1917 the local newspaper was able to describe the museum's free library as containing books on all facets of science as well as a large selection of magazines.

Reverend Bragg's continued correspondence ignited a strong interest in poetry in his daughter, which led to more interaction with some of her literary friends in Charleston such as noted novelists and poets Josephine Pinckney and DuBose Heyward. In 1919 they, along with three others, formed the Poetry Society of South Carolina, which became an important player in the literary and cultural renaissance that was beginning to emerge in the city. It also provided another venue of influential and financial support for the museum and Bragg's community projects.

When Dr. Rea left The Charleston Museum to take a position in Cleveland, Laura Bragg was named director. In October 1920 she became the first woman in the United States to lead a publicly supported museum—and the oldest one in the country at that. Soon thereafter she opened the museum's doors to blacks for the first time on Saturday afternoons. By March she had established a free children's library that allowed the lending of books to all children under eighteen and to teachers in the county. By the end of her first year as director she wrote to her father, "I have never worked so hard in my life—every hour full. But, oh, it is grand to be getting results. We have done more at the museum this year than in any three or four before." It must have been a source of pride, if she had the time to consider it, that attendance at the museum had increased from a count of 10,000 visitors during 1910 to nearly 39,000 in 1920.

In 1923, to celebrate the 150th anniversary of The Charleston Museum's founding, Bragg lured the American Association of Museums to hold its annual meeting in Charleston. With The Charleston Museum serving as the headquarters, Bragg worked tirelessly to coordinate all aspects of the meeting and social events showcasing the sites of historic Charleston. With the help of her numerous contacts and prominent friends, the event was a huge success that garnered additional recognition for Bragg's adopted city and the museum.

More accolades followed for her as a result such as committee membership on the Woman's Bureau of the Charleston Chamber of Commerce, membership on one of the national committees of the American Association of Museums, and publication of her biography in the first edition of *Women in America*. Not one to rest on praise, she opened a South Carolina Culture Gallery in the museum to preserve and foster understanding of the state's cultural history. As Charleston grew to become a tourist destination, which revitalized her economy, more of the city's leadership recognized the need to preserve her heritage both locally and statewide. Bragg investigated the native Sewee Indian tribe, collected Negro folklore, purchased Edgefield pottery (a unique utilitarian stoneware produced in the Edgefield District of South Carolina), and explored rice cultivation as some of the topics important to the state's diverse cultural influences. She also joined forces with the Society for the Preservation of Old Dwellings (the forerunner of today's Preservation Society of Charleston) to raise funds, purchase, and preserve the Heyward-Washington House, a historic property where George Washington stayed during his Southern Tour as President in 1791.

At the same time she refined her focus on interpreting the natural history and lives of other people around the world. Through her presentations of cultural material, she wanted to:

> create, among our own people, a better understanding and appreciation of foreign peoples. . . . Conditions are so changed as to bring us into closer contact with peoples throughout the world, and for our own ultimate good, require closer understanding . . . appreciation, and sympathy, through knowledge, are so far as the human mind has yet discovered the best means of making them [wars] as infrequent as possible.

Bragg's concept of what she now referred to as a "culture history museum" was spread through another outlet when she was asked by Columbia University in 1925 to teach a course in museum administration at their summer session. For the next three summers she eagerly worked to train the students to fill the growing need for professional museum workers and to foster her own ideas of museum service among those already working in smaller museums.

Back at home Bragg continued to push for a public library with her ally Mayor Stoney. Through her museum contacts, the Rosewald Fund of Chicago pledged financial support to a free library for the county with the stipulation that matching funds must come from the local delegation. The Charleston legislators initially did not support it in the Depression era of extremely tight funds but eventually reconsidered after numerous civic groups and community leaders convinced them of the pressing need. Bragg's dream of a free library was finally realized when it opened at the museum on January 1, 1931, and she became incorporator, trustee, and librarian. Within six months the nearby communities of Mt. Pleasant, McClellanville, St. Paul's Parish, and Edisto Island opened branch libraries, and a private library serving the black community called Dart Hall all became part of the Charleston County Library system.

Feeling much satisfaction from her accomplishments with The Charleston Museum and the community, Bragg began to seek out new challenges. In the spring of 1931 she was approached by industrialist Zenas Marshall Crane to reorganize his family's art museum into an educational and cultural institution. The Berkshire Museum was located in Pittsfield, Massachusetts, at the foot of the Berkshire Mountains and was entirely funded by generous gifts from Crane family members. Over the next eight years, Bragg instituted a lot of changes and generated some controversy too. She installed numerous modern art exhibits and educational programs that received national publicity in the *New Yorker,* the *New York Times,* and *Art Digest.* She was the first to exhibit the work of Alfred Maurer,

Alexander Calder, and other young artists struggling during the bleak years of the Depression. She undertook the renovation, redecoration, and expansion of the facility as well. She woke up what Crane called "his old man's attic of a museum" into a place of learning and discovery attractive to both the ordinary citizen and the culturally, if conservative-minded, elite. Attendance after her first year at the helm was more than double the average attendance for the previous years.

In 1939 Bragg retired to Charleston, where she lived a life of contemplative study and teaching. Drawing on her vast depth of knowledge, she lectured to a devoted following of young people in morning classes held in her home on Chalmers Street. She also hosted Sunday evening salons, leading lively discussions for the literary and artistic members of the community. She often entertained notable visitors to Charleston and invited them to the Sunday gatherings—including Robert Frost, who read his poetry to the group. Until her death at the age of ninety-six in May 1978, Laura Bragg was considered the Grand Dame of Charleston, a status befitting the intelligent, innovative, and progressive feminist who not only cherished and enriched her own city but also influenced the direction of museums across the country.

MARIE CROMER SEIGLER

1882–1964

Girls' Club Founder

BEFORE SHE KNEW IT, MARIE CROMER had leapt to her feet in the middle of a presentation. Attending the state teachers' meeting in Columbia during the Christmas holidays of 1909, Marie had listened intently to the information delivered by O. B. Martin, a U.S. Department of Agriculture representative, about the Boys' Corn Clubs of America. He described and praised the work of the clubs and their successes in agricultural production, as well as the wonderful influences that the clubs had had on the boys' lives. (Boys' Corn Clubs, to improve the quality and yield of the corn crop, were first established in the Midwest and had emerged in South Carolina by 1908.) Marie couldn't wait any longer to ask the presenter about the possibility of something similar being offered to girls. When he countered by asking "Why don't you organize a club for the girls?" she replied, "If that is what you are waiting for, I will certainly do it." At that moment she knew she had found her calling; she would take on the challenge and create an opportunity for the girls back home on the farms in Aiken County.

Later, explaining her vision to help broaden the lives of girls and young women in rural farming communities, Marie Cromer said, "I was born in the country. I live in the country, and I know something of its lonesomeness and sleepy-spiritedness. It is because I love the country and its people that I want to do something for the young girls—to help them keep the thinking up when school is over."

Marie Samuella was born to Ella Cox and William Oscar Cromer on November 9, 1882, in rural Abbeville County, South Carolina. She was raised along with her eight siblings on a farm on Clover Hill Plantation—land that had been in her family for four generations. Her doting father nicknamed the petite Marie "Beaut," short for "Beautiful," and encouraged her self-confidence and ambitions. Even as a young girl she wanted to make a difference somehow for her generation; she kept that goal in mind throughout her schooling. She attended Smithville Township's one-teacher school and then Abbeville High School, graduating in 1898. She pursued further education at a small college in North Carolina and returned to South Carolina to teach for several years in Greenwood and Saluda County schools. By 1907 she moved to Aiken County to begin a job teaching at Talatha School and serve as the county representative of the School Improvement Association (which later became the Parent–Teachers Association). She boarded with the Seigler family at their home in Eureka, South Carolina (first known as Seigler's Crossing). Also within the household was Cecil Hodges Seigler, the superintendent of education for Aiken County Schools, the son of the owners. Cecil and Marie would marry some years later on April 24, 1912.

In 1901 the United States Department of Agriculture (USDA) had begun a nationwide effort under the leadership of Dr. Seaman A. Knapp to disseminate information on modern farming techniques. He was pioneering demonstrations of better agricultural practices on local farms around the country through the Office of the Farmers' Cooperative Demonstration Work. He, and his state agents like O. B. Martin, also hoped to foster and organize national clubs for training young people who might be more receptive to new farming ideas than their parents.

Especially in the economically depressed post-Reconstruction South, advances in agriculture and domestic life had not kept up with other parts of the country. South Carolina was an agricultural state made up of mainly small, one-family farms. These farming families existed on what they raised or produced on their own farm. What income was generated from their single cash crop was stretched among seed, fertilizer, and equipment for the farm, and then the family's needs of clothing, and other canned and dry goods, and, lastly, health care. The farm's labor force consisted of the family members with sons and daughters working in the fields as soon as their age allowed. Conveniences such as running water and electricity were rare. Methods of farming were still based upon information handed down from father to son, and domestic skills were passed from mother to daughter. The basics of sanitation, nutrition, health, and home economics were often unknown. As a rural schoolteacher Marie had witnessed the signs of hunger and malnutrition, such as pellagra and low energy levels, in many of her students. She sought a way to address the problem in her own community. A better diet throughout the year was a way to start. She heard of a plan for growing tomatoes and then safely canning them for consumption all year long. Perhaps she could devise a program that would teach her pupils the proper methods for achieving this.

Shortly after that pivotal teachers' meeting, Marie single-handedly undertook organizing a Girls' Tomato Club, working after her school day was done on nights and weekends for several months. She consulted her husband-to-be, Cecil Seigler, in mapping out some of the plans. Superintendent of Education Seigler was also in charge of the Aiken County Boys' Corn Club.

He advised Marie on details such as the size of the plot the girls should work and what achievements would merit prizes. He also talked up her new club while visiting area schools. In addition to what she could gather from books, Marie requested and received information from the USDA on growing tomatoes that she could share with the young girls. Initially, she found her efforts met with apathy, ridicule, and even opposition, but she persevered. She wrote letters to parents and the community newspapers and visited girls in their homes and schools around the county. To attract more interest Marie knew that she needed a really good prize to offer. She enticed them with a chance for a one-year scholarship to Winthrop College, the women's college in Spartanburg, South Carolina. The scholarship would be awarded to the girl who demonstrated the best record in cultivating and preserving tomatoes. Other prizes were offered for the largest yield, largest net gain, best display in glass jars, largest tomato, and best record-keeping of her cultivation experience. Any girl in the county between the ages of nine and twenty-two could join the club. She was allowed help in preparing the soil for her garden, but otherwise all the work planting and tending a one-tenth acre plot of tomatoes was her sole responsibility.

The first Aiken County Girls' Tomato Club numbered twelve charter members and finally had forty-seven girls enrolled from several Aiken County Schools by the spring planting season in 1910. This marked the first group of its kind in the nation. While the girls cultivated their tomato crops on each of their designated one-tenth-acre plots, Marie worked to secure the funds for the boldly promised $140 scholarship. At the time this was a large sum for her to raise, considering she made only $40 a month at her teaching job. She realized that even with tight budgeting she would be unable to donate enough funds herself by the start of Winthrop's fall session, so she decided to approach some of Aiken's wealthy winter residents such as Mr. John D. Rockefeller, Mrs. Russell Sage, and Miss Helen Gould. At first there was no response to this plea, but finally Mr. Thomas Hitchcock, another winter resident, stepped forward to underwrite the scholarship. Marie, fearful but determined that her endeavor should not fail, was elated with this commitment. Soon afterward, the South Carolina General Assembly pledged to fund the scholarship, lending even more credibility to her new organization.

As the girls' crops matured, Marie left for New England in the summer of 1910. She was sent there by the USDA to observe the latest techniques in food preparation, specifically the art of canning in tin and other domestic sciences. She frequently wrote letters to her girls to encourage them and keep up their enthusiasm. In one letter she wrote:

> Dear Little Tomato Girl,
> . . . Be sure your garden measurements are correct. They should be 4,356 feet or 66 feet square. In trying for the $5.00 prize for the best "Tomato book," use good grade drawing paper about 9" x 1". Make an attractive cover. . . . Use water-color prints and draw in tomatoes . . . . Of course you will discuss the life and history of tomatoes and of the Aiken County Girls' Tomato Club. . . . The remainder of your book will have facts that will help a tomato grower. Your book will be judged on neatness, usefulness, beauty, and handwriting. . . . Aiken is a great county and you are going to make it greater . . .

In Marie's absence Superintendent Seigler did what he could to assist the club. He even sponsored and oversaw the first canning demonstration for girls held in the small community of Windsor, South Carolina. John D. Rockefeller had come to their aid this time by donating the canning machine to the Tomato Club. The

USDA was also very involved, having the canning outfit sent by train from Illinois and providing three thousand cans and labels bearing the inscription "South Carolina Tomatoes. Grown and packed by the Aiken County Girls' Tomato Club." Winthrop College sent a special instructor to help the girls in the canning process. In July, O. B. Martin organized a three-day canning bee held in front of the Aiken County courthouse where each step of the process was demonstrated. Paring, scalding, and filling the cans with tomatoes was followed by capping and soldering, then boiling the filled cans, removing and labeling them—all carefully observed not only by the girls' mothers but many other interested onlookers. Some of the girls' brothers, often members of a corn club, gathered wood to help keep the fires stoked for the boiling water. By the end of the three days, one of the charter tomato club members, fourteen-year-old Katie Gunter of the Samaria community near Wagener, whom "we all remember as having made a record never before equaled" was the winner. "She filled 512 No. 3 cans with tomatoes from her one-tenth acre," recalled Marie, and Katie collected the staggering sum of $40 in sales in addition to her scholarship prize.

At the end of the first canning season Marie wrote a column that expressed her deep pride in the girls' accomplishments.

> . . . The interest that each little girl has manifested in her garden has not been superficial. It has been real, spontaneous, vital. This Club does not stand for simply the raising of tomatoes. It stands for lessons economic and lessons ethical. From the cultivation of their gardens have arisen problems of soil, drainage, pests, rotation of crops and of actual money values, of obeying laws, working together for a common need, taking failure, and making success from it, and last but not least, the unselfish acknowledgement of others' success . . .

A few months ago this Club was so new till little girls were afraid to join it. They were not quite sure that it was the right thing. Today it stands upon its own merits having received the approbation of the people, club women, organizations, the press, and the Department of Agriculture of the United States.

This Club has awakened in the girls an interest in growing things—has made them want to know more about plants and how to cultivate them; it has given them a feeling of satisfaction in the results of their own labor; it has helped to train them in habits of economy and industry; finally, it has developed in their young minds a taste for outdoor life, a love of nature, and a desire to know more about "the great, wide, beautiful, wonderful world" in which we live . . .

For the rest of the summer, O. B. Martin took the large canner (compared in size to a two-horse wagon) to communities around the state for more public canning bees. The demonstrations evolved into community events attended by large numbers of people. In addition to the instruction and production of canned fruits and vegetables, picnics and socializing added to the success of the project. Martin returned to Washington and enthusiastically reported on how popular the canning bees had become:

> . . . the girls take a great deal of pride and interest in their plants
> . . . the [USDA] circulars were carefully studied. A great deal
> was being learned about the soil and plants, by growing and
> studying one plant . . . they [the instructors] could make many
> valuable suggestions with regard to sanitation, hygiene and gen-
> eral home improvement after having secured the confidence and
> good will of the girls and their mothers through the club.
> . . . It can be readily seen that when this work develops
> it will have a far-reaching effect. It will affect the homes in
> an economic way because the girls can convert some of their

spare time into profit. It will encourage thrift. It will also lead to various lines of home improvement. The well trained and enthusiastic young woman working in a county, can bring about wonderful changes in a year. It will have a fine educational value and a beneficial reflex influence on the schools.

The USDA responded quickly to expand the canning clubs to other parts of the South. By the end of the year Virginia, Tennessee, and Mississippi had home demonstration agents initiating canning clubs with funds that Knapp garnered through the General Education Board of New York City and his own Farmers' Cooperative Demonstration Work Office. The General Education Board gave the clubs $25,000 for equipment, and the Department of Agriculture provided publicity and instructional materials with another $5,000. Marie became the president of the Rural School Improvement Association of Aiken County and State Organizer of Girls' Tomato Clubs in South Carolina. She traveled the state spreading word about the clubs and seeking money for more scholarships. She worked continuously to improve the clubs with more learning opportunities for the girls. On August 16, 1910, the USDA appointed Marie a special state agent, and within a year she had set up and enrolled 3,000 members in Girls' Tomato Clubs. At the National Corn Show held in Columbia in late 1910, a joint exhibit was set up by the Girls' Tomato Club and the Boys' Corn Club of Aiken County. Under the guidance of Marie Cromer and Cecil Seigler this collaboration marked the first time the two groups had worked together and eventually would lead to the merger that formed the 4-H Clubs of America.

By 1912 Marie's fledgling concept had grown to more than 23,000 canning clubs across the South. With the passage of the federal Smith-Lever Act in 1914 (co-authored by South Carolina Congressman A. F. Lever) the work was consolidated under the land-grant colleges in each state, specifically Clemson College for South Carolina. By 1929, South Carolina, in cooperation with the

USDA and county governments, had a home demonstration agent in every county.

Upon Marie's marriage to Cecil Seigler in April 1912, she proudly wore a diamond sunburst pin on her bridal veil that she had received from Aiken County in recognition and appreciation of the work she had done. The couple received a cut glass bowl with a silver band around the top as a wedding gift from the USDA that has since been handed down as a treasured family heirloom. As was the norm then, most women did not work outside the home once they were married. Marie carried on her work for a short time, resigning on July 31 so that a new appointment could be made before school began in the fall. She quietly turned her attention to becoming a homemaker and later mother to a son and a daughter at the Seiglers' home in Eureka. She had the satisfaction of knowing that her dream of improving the health, self-confidence, and domestic skills of her farming community girls had taken on a widespread awareness and was beginning to broaden horizons for young women on a national scale.

After a lengthy illness and hospitalization, Marie Cromer Seigler enjoyed some recognition in her later years for her groundbreaking efforts. In 1953 President Dwight D. Eisenhower presented her with a gold medallion and a National 4-H Camp Citation, a citation noting "Certain selected persons, who, over a period of years have made distinct contributions to the nation-wide development of the 4-H Club Program." She died on June 14, 1964, and is buried in her husband's family cemetery between Eureka and Johnston, South Carolina. Seven college scholarships are given in memory of Marie Seigler by the Anderson, Orangeburg, Darlington, and Aiken County Councils of Farm Women. She was inducted posthumously into the Greater Abbeville Chamber of Commerce's Hall of Fame in 1985 and their offices contain a portrait of her.

At a 4-H rally in Columbia in 1938, U.S. senator James F. Byrnes stated, "The pioneer spirit of Mrs. Seigler has resulted in the organization of girls' clubs in every state of the union. That this young woman's efforts were the origin of the 4-H clubs is a source of great pride to all South Carolinians." Today, there are 4-H programs in every county, state, and territory, and the District of Columbia, as well as many foreign countries. The organization includes a multitude of educational experiences developing leadership, citizenship, and life skills involving more than seven million American youths.

WIL LOU GRAY

1883-1984

Pioneer Educator

YOUNG, IDEALISTIC WIL LOU GRAY came bounding into her Uncle Will's home office bubbling over with her day's accomplishments at Wallace Lodge School. She could hardly wait to share with him her success of teaching her young pupils "the three Rs" and how quickly they were progressing. She stopped in her tracks suddenly when she realized that someone was already in the room. It was one of her uncle's tenant farmers settling an account with him. She watched from the doorway as the farmer made a mark to denote a signature since he was unable to sign his name. She was quite taken aback. Surely everyone had been to school and knew how to read and write. Naively it had never occurred to her that grown people could be uneducated. She would never forget this moment, and it would have a profound influence on her thoughts in the years ahead.

Wil Lou Gray was born on August 29, 1883, in Laurens, South Carolina. She was the middle child of William Lafayette Gray and Sarah Louise Dial, who gave their daughter her unusual dual name from each of theirs, "Wil" shortened from William and "Lou" from

Wil Lou Gray, shown here ca. 1918, tackled illiteracy statewide through the South Carolina Illiteracy Commission.

Louise. Many said it foreshadowed her dual personality traits of a man's keen business sense and a woman's maternal compassion. Her mother died when Wil Lou was only nine years old, but her father later remarried, and Wil Lou was fortunate to gain a devoted step-mother. William Gray was a prominent businessman in Laurens, and she and her two brothers were raised in a comfortable, caring environment.

After graduation from Laurens High School in 1899, Wil Lou attended Columbia College in Columbia, South Carolina, attaining her degree in 1903. After graduation her parents discouraged her from working, preferring her to live at home and enjoy a pleasant, easy lifestyle, as was the custom for most young unmarried women of means in her day. But Wil Lou was too energetic to take that route. Instead she planned to earn a living teaching, just as many of her fellow classmates were doing. A teaching career offered one of the few acceptable ways that a genteel woman could have an occupation in that time of limited opportunity for women. That summer Wil Lou persuaded her father to let her attend a summer session at Winthrop College, South Carolina's State Normal School for Women, to further develop her practical teaching skills. She had already accepted a position at the Jones School, a one-teacher school in nearby Wares Shoals in Greenwood County. At the summer session she studied under Annie Bonham, who offered some progressive ideas new in the field. Bonham emphasized that a teacher should know her community and learn about the family background of each of her pupils.

Wil Lou took this advice to heart and set out to meet the townspeople of Ware Shoals. She attended church on Sundays and spent Saturdays calling on each of the families of her students. From her upbringing she knew to wear her best attire when "calling," so on that first outing she selected a high-necked, long silk dress with a stiff whale-boned waist. It also had a train as was the style of the day. She laced up her high heels and soon discovered how inappropriate her outfit was for walking over the dusty, red-earthed hills. The train was reduced to tatters when an unattended dog chased her and tore it as she ran away. Although she may have chosen the wrong clothing, her intentions were clear, and she was received with open arms into her new community.

She met the challenge of teaching all levels from beginners through high school. She conveyed a love of literature and poetry, and taught her students to recite favorite verses. She developed hands-on projects such as map-making, in which her pupils stayed after school to construct brown paper maps molding mountains from wet newspapers and coloring them with dye to depict world geography. She organized social activities, too, such as a candy pulling and a book club for adults encouraging reading among the parents of her pupils. Tapping into a new State Library Law providing partial funding for school libraries, she acquired the other appropriations needed to establish a new library for the Jones School. By the end of that first year, Wil Lou knew she had found her life's calling and embraced the opportunity to achieve more.

The following year she moved to another one-teacher school, Wallace Lodge in Laurens County. Initially she had only nine pupils, but after the cotton crop was picked in late fall, attendance jumped to sixty-five. Another teacher was hired to teach the lower grades while Wil Lou concentrated on the high school–level children. While teaching there she was able to live at the home of her Uncle Will Harris, a household including Mr. and Mrs. Harris, their nine children, household staff, and frequent guests. This was a lively and stimulating home for Wil Lou, and, at the same time, living in another rural setting gave her new insight into the limitations of people who had never been taught to read and write.

After another year at Wallace Lodge, Wil Lou decided to return to school herself, and she entered graduate school at

Vanderbilt University in the fall of 1905. It was a rich experience for her, inspiring more devotion to her profession in the spirit of giving back to her community and state. She planned to teach on the college level, but she was lured back to Wallace Lodge, which was now called Young's School, with the promise of an assistant teacher in a brand-new two-room schoolhouse.

Demonstrating her resourcefulness, Wil Lou rallied the community behind her effort to win a $100 prize given to ten South Carolina schools showing the most physical improvement in one year. The new school was unpainted, so she collected the money to buy the paint and then urged everyone from school trustees to parents to pupils to help paint the building. Time was short so they painted only two sides, which were carefully shown in the winning photograph submitted, and the other sides were painted later.

Wil Lou wanted to add music to the school curriculum to broaden her students' education. She asked her father for some of the brick from a commercial building he was tearing down so that she could trade the old brick for a used organ. From an early age, Wil Lou Gray was never daunted by obstacles to her goals; she just worked that much harder to make them become reality.

In 1907, Wil Lou became a college professor at a girls' school in Abbington, Virginia, called Martha Washington College. She taught English and enjoyed the atmosphere of collegial life, but deep down she knew her heart was with the rural people back home who needed her more. Again she sought more training to serve them better. In 1910 she entered Columbia University, where she earned her Master of Arts in Political Science in June 1911. Still a bit torn about her future, she deliberated over a choice between teaching history at the college level for more pay or returning to Laurens and accepting a position as supervisor of Laurens County schools with long hours at the low pay of $50 a month. Consulting her family, one relative asked a pertinent question, "Wouldn't you

like to make history? You can do that here in Laurens County."
That question hit its mark.

Wil Lou dove into her new responsibilities as the supervisor of
the Laurens County schools. She would leave home every Monday
morning traveling by horse and buggy and not return home until
Friday night. She spent her days visiting the schools, afternoons
meeting with the teachers, and evenings holding community meetings. Her nights were spent in the homes of hospitable parents. She
used the time with them to encourage their sending their children
to school (stressing the need for regular attendance in the agricultural county) and on to college.

She outlined many objectives for the Laurens County schools,
which included better prepared teachers through in-service training, attendance at state teachers' meetings, and membership in state
and national teachers' organizations. She persuaded many leading
South Carolina college educators to come to her schools as speakers
for the students, teachers, and parents, often driving them herself
from one school to another on poor roads that sometimes took
hours to cover a distance of only a few miles. She even wrote her
own teaching materials when she could not find what she considered suitable; *A Synopsis of South Carolina History* issued by the
Laurens County Department of Education in 1914 was one of her
printed bulletins used by the schools. Other initiatives were a plea
for improved facilities and two new school buildings to include
outhouses. She lobbied for raising taxes to help accomplish this
goal. She wanted to see that every child was enrolled in school and
regularly attended. One man even confessed that he would rather
send his children to school than have Miss Wil Lou come see him
if they were absent. Her resolve was further evident when she
logged more than a thousand miles in her buggy to get the necessary petition signatures for mandatory school attendance. She instituted a uniform seventh-grade examination and a public awarding

of completion certificates to the students. This resulted in greater numbers of children feeling a sense of achievement and continuing on through high school instead of dropping out as many had previously done at that point.

While driving those many miles around the county, Wil Lou had time to think and plan even bigger things. The image of the tenant farmer "making his mark" kept coming back to mind. Her work had further confirmed the large numbers of illiterate adults in the rural communities, and she felt that something had to be done to combat the problem. In 1915 she drafted a report to the State Superintendent of Education entitled "A Night School Experiment in Laurens County, South Carolina." It was agreed that she would set up and conduct a trial of a night school in Young's Township, which had a very large number of land owners and tenant farmers who had not had the benefit of formal education. To relieve any reluctance about admitting their lack of education to others, Wil Lou also organized advanced classes for the more educated so that a joint learning environment was created. Easing her uncertainty about how it would be received, one tenant farmer told her that he would gladly give half of his crop that year if he could learn to read and write. He also volunteered to drive others in his wagon to attend the new classes.

Despite a heavy downpour on the first night twenty-one people showed up eager to learn. After the study plan for the evening was outlined, they had only one request—that the ten-minute intermission between classes be eliminated so that they would have more time for instruction. In short order, six more night schools were started with day-school teachers volunteering their time. Word spread and attendance soared. Each night Wil Lou traveled to one school, no matter what the weather, setting an example for the adult students. At the Young's School, which had 137 students, all the beginners learned to write their names and read a little.

Some were able to compose letters and work primary arithmetic. The trustees wrote that "we cannot recommend the night school too highly to any community having adults who cannot read and write, and we believe it will help the cause of education in any community."

Even with this success and a few other scattered efforts in other counties around the state, no state support was forthcoming for the program. Public indifference so discouraged Wil Lou Gray that she resigned her position and returned to Columbia University for more study. While there she received an attractive offer to become supervisor of rural schools in Montgomery County, Maryland, considered one of the most educationally progressive counties in the country. Perhaps needing a respite from the uphill struggles of support for her programs at home, Wil Lou accepted the job.

But world political events began to intervene, bringing more attention to the adult illiteracy problem. World War I drew national focus on the numbers of soldiers, black and white, poor and privileged, who could not write or read letters from home. Stories emerged that illustrated the poignancy of situations like that told of a soldier too proud to admit that he couldn't read a letter he received. He carried it around for months before getting the courage to ask someone to read it to him, and when it was read, he learned for the first time of his newborn son back home. Alarmed by this situation, the State Federation of Women's Clubs organized a citizens' meeting in Columbia in January 1918. After further discussion of the seriousness of the problem, they asked Governor Manning to establish a State Illiteracy Commission, which he promptly did. The first appointed commission received no public funding and quickly became overwhelmed with the monumental task and dispersed. A second commission was selected and accepted the challenge in June 1918, immediately seeking donations from individuals and the State Council of Defense. With this seed money they hoped to appeal to the General Assembly for an appropriation to carry on the work permanently. They also knew that they needed an outstanding, dynamic, and experienced individual to lead the new effort. The clear choice was Wil Lou Gray.

Though she had only spent one year in her job in Maryland, Gray was intrigued by the opportunity to continue the work she had begun on a larger, statewide basis. Realizing that she was giving up a secure job with good compensation for one that was uncertain with no commitment of financial support from the legislature must have given her pause. But she returned to South Carolina in 1918 ready to tackle a new set of obstacles. As Executive Secretary for the South Carolina Illiteracy Commission she summoned her constructive energy and enthusiasm, public service idealism, and trained educational background to awaken South Carolina to the seriousness of the problem. The national derogatory comment "as illiterate as South Carolina" weighed heavily on her and reflected the reality that the state had the highest adult illiteracy rate in the country at that time. She took her campaign across the state, speaking to every group and organization that would hear her urging that the state must educate South Carolinians for South Carolina. She spread the message that the state could not rise above the level of her own uneducated citizens.

At the same time she trained teachers and set up all kinds of adult schools to meet the needs of each community across the state. She convinced cotton mill owners to hire full-time teachers with salaries paid jointly by the mill and the state to teach the workers in their mill villages. In tobacco-growing areas lantern-lit tobacco barns served as school rooms while the tobacco cured. Other "lay-by schools" were organized when farmers and their families had the time to attend between cultivation and harvest. Adult schools were set up in every county in crossroad stores, country churches, and community buildings, reaching out to black and white. Recognizing this innovative work the State Department of Education established a Department of Adult Education with Wil Lou Gray becoming the first Adult Education Director for South Carolina.

Not content to rest on these accomplishments, a new experiment was taking shape in her thoughts. Gray wanted to create a school where a more intensive course of instruction could be taught full-time to adults who could leave home for four weeks to attend. She would find a site vacant in the summer months where her undereducated adults could enjoy a semblance of college life with a simplified academic curriculum tailored to their needs. The "Opportunity School" was born when the Daughters of the American Revolution (DAR) loaned their camp in Tamassee, in the foothills of northwest South Carolina, for this purpose. On August 2, 1921, seventeen young women, all over the age of fourteen with no education beyond the fifth grade, registered as boarding students, and nineteen men signed up for night classes. In addition to the basics of reading and writing, citizenship, good health habits, manners, and domestic science were taught.

The experiment proved to be a success; then came the task of expanding with more funding and support. That fall the Upper South Carolina Methodist Conference committed funds and their women's college campus, Lander College, with the state furnishing the salary for the teachers. The South Carolina Baptist Convention also aided the effort by providing its academy at Lyman, South Carolina, for a campus for men. In 1922, eighty-nine women attended at Lander College ranging in age from fourteen to fifty-one. The school operated on a shoestring with the women doing most of the domestic work to keep down expenses. Gossett Mills in Anderson sent twenty women from their four mills, paying their way while preserving their jobs. Mr. James P. Gossett was so pleased with the results that he sent twenty male workers the following year to the men's Opportunity School now held at Erskine College in Due

West and continued his patronage until the Depression years. The first men's group numbered seventy-two pupils, and the school stayed at Erskine until 1930. In 1925 the women's school moved to Anderson College, due to remodeling taking place at Lander. Renovations at Anderson College forced another move in 1928 to the Women's College in Due West. Miss Gray kept up her campaign to solicit scholarship money to help more adult students have the benefit of the learning experience. As she recounted the numerous success stories of her pupils who became not only better workers but better citizens in just a month, more support came in and notable faculty were attracted. The faculty included Margaret Tolbert, future Adult Education Director for South Carolina; J. M. Lesesne, future president of Erskine; and J. Strom Thurmond, future U.S. senator.

In 1931 the Opportunity School became co-educational and moved to Clemson College, conducting its one-month sessions there until 1942. Ever resourceful, Miss Gray persuaded Clemson authorities to offer up a vacant lot where she spearheaded the funding and construction of a demonstration house for $1,500. The Opportunity students then made the furniture, curtains, bedspreads, and other furnishings as part of their course work. The house was named Opphame and served as part of ongoing home economics classes. It was rented in the winter months to a Clemson professor, adding to scholarship funds for more Opportunity School students. Miss Gray's frugal budgeting enabled many of her students whom had never left their communities to go on "pilgrimages," as she called them, to see educational sights within the state at Charleston and Columbia and away to Washington, D.C., and New York. At the same time, an Opportunity School for Negroes was set up at Seneca Junior College in Seneca, South Carolina. In an era of divisive bigotry, Miss Gray forged ahead, championing the cause of equal education for both races. The same year the school was a recipient of a Carnegie Foundation grant of $10,000 to study the learning ability of adults.

The findings concluded that adults learn faster than children, whites and blacks learn equally, and the more education one has the easier it is to learn. This study confirmed the validity of Miss Gray's work.

During the upheaval of the war years of World War II, the Opportunity Schools had to relocate again, fostering a desire for a more permanent home. As many veterans returned from the war, the state acknowledged the need for more educational efforts directed toward its adult population. An appropriation of $65,000 was made for Miss Gray to obtain 998 acres and 200 buildings at the deactivated Columbia Air Base for a year-round school. It opened on January 2, 1947, and was expanded to accommodate day and evening as well as boarding students. The mission remained focused on an academic education combined with practical skills for every-day life summed up in the school's motto, "Why Stop Learning?"

In the twenty-eight years that Wil Lou Gray served as State Supervisor of Adult Education, more than 275,000 adults attended their local community schools. From 1910 to 1950 South Carolina's adult illiteracy rate dropped from 25.7 to 5.3 percent, in part due to her innovative programs. Wil Lou Gray retired in 1957, but her legacy of the community and Opportunity schools goes on to meet the needs of South Carolinians. She lived to be one hundred and spent the rest of her years actively volunteering for numerous causes, most notably establishing the South Carolina Federation on Aging (now known as the South Carolina Council on Aging), giving a voice to senior citizens.

As praise and recognition were bestowed upon her in later years, she characteristically responded, "I've had tremendous support in all my endeavors. Anyone can do what I have done. You know, I'm not very smart and I never have been able to spell."

Her portrait hangs in the South Carolina State House, paying tribute to a life dedicated to creating more educational opportunities for all South Carolinians.

LILY STRICKLAND ANDERSON

1884-1958

American Composer

EVEN MODEST LILY STRICKLAND ANDERSON had to acknowledge that her "li'l banjo song," as she called it, had hit the big time. Here she was halfway around the world in the lobby of a grand hotel in Shanghai, China, and the orchestra was playing "Mah Lindy Lou" as she walked in. Her little song, which she had scribbled down quickly one afternoon in her apartment in New York in a wave of homesickness, had come to her quickly. The three verses had spilled out, and she never changed a word or note of it afterward. As she would often relate the story, it was January 1920, and she and her husband were just about to leave the country to move to India, and she was thinking fondly of home. Home always meant the Deep South and her childhood home of Anderson, South Carolina—a home she knew she would not see again for many years.

Lily Strickland was born in Anderson on January 28, 1884. She was the only daughter of Charlton Hines Strickland and Teresa Hammond Reed. The family lived with her maternal grandparents, Judge and Mrs. J. Pinckney Reed at Echo Hall, described by *The State* newspaper in 1958 as "a beautiful old place in the midst of

Lily Strickland enjoyed much success during her prolific career.

formal gardens." The home was built by Judge Reed, whom the paper went on to portray as "a man of such great personal charm and ability that his legend persists after six generations. He is remembered as an immaculate dresser, who wore frock-coat and stove-pipe hat and carried a gold-headed cane. Yet he often 'fiddled', as he called it, for dances at his house when his many daughters were young, and is said to have been full of fun and frolic." In addition to his distinguished career as a judge, he was a successful lawyer, publisher of Anderson's first newspaper, and a member of the South Carolina Secession Convention. Lily's grandmother was also known for her friendliness and charm, and both grandparents provided strong influences on Lily Strickland's childhood.

For a brief time the family relocated to New York City, where Lily's father's work as an insurance salesman had taken them. But upon her father's death a few years later, Lily and her two brothers returned with their mother to Echo Hall. Often sung to sleep by her mother and aunt, Lily was surrounded by a musical, and warm, loving family. She attended local Anderson schools and began learning to play the piano at the age of six. At an even younger age, her family reminisced that she would stretch up on tiptoes, barely reaching the keyboard, to pick out a few notes of musical expression. As a small child she often listened to the cotton pickers as they sang while working in the nearby fields. Absorbing the Negro rhythm and melodies and the other influences of the natural environment of long Southern days amidst the pines and magnolias and the chirping of songbirds provided Lily with inspiration for her first compositions. Her older cousin Reed Miller, a noted concert tenor, encouraged her by singing the songs she made up. Other family members fostered her musical ambitions as well, and Lily played the pipe organ in the local Episcopal church and published her first compositions when she was only sixteen.

Lily received her formal musical education at Converse College in Spartanburg, South Carolina, known across the South for its strong music program. There she studied piano and composition from 1901 to 1904. In 1905 she received a scholarship for study at the Institute of Musical Art in New York, a forerunner to the Julliard School of Music. For the next several years she studied piano, orchestration, theory, and composition at the school. At a first meeting with one of her teachers, Alfred Goodrich, she noticed on his music rack one of her own compositions, which he was using as a model of form for his other students.

While living in New York, accompanied by her mother, she met her husband-to-be. One day, her mother was returning to their apartment and was unable to open the door because it had become stuck. She sought help from a graduate student who lived in the same building. When he opened the door, they found Lily playing the piano. They learned that the young man was also a teacher at Columbia University and a fellow South Carolinian from the Piedmont area. An immediate friendship was born. In 1912 Lily married Joseph Courtenay Anderson.

While Courtenay continued his graduate work and teaching, Lily began to gain some attention for her compositions. Reflecting the influence of her Southern roots, her black dialect songs, "Honey Chile," "Pickaninny Sleep Song," "Mah Rose," "Lonesome Moonlight," and "Hear Dem Bells," as well as some of her piano suites, demonstrated her intimate knowledge of Negro speech and rhythmic expression. Her musical training and skill enabled her to convey this understanding into popular music and verse.

During World War I Courtenay Anderson was stationed at Camp MacArthur in Waco, Texas, where he served as education director. Lily soon involved herself in the war effort there too, serving as a volunteer with the YMCA, providing musical entertainment for the troops. She also expressed the country's patriotic fervor with her wartime songs "America Victorious," "To a Highlander," and "To Our Allied Dead." She taught music and continued to compose, with much of her work at that time inspired by the southwestern influences of the American Indian and Mexican cultures. In her travels with her husband to Kansas, Oklahoma, and New Mexico, she captured the spirit of the region in her compositions "Two Shawnee Indian Dances" and "Sketches of the Southwest."

The next chapter of Lily's life began in 1920 when Courtenay accepted a position with an import business that relocated the couple to Calcutta, India. Over the next nine and a half years they embraced their surroundings and used the opportunity to travel extensively not only throughout India but also to Ceylon (Sri Lanka), Burma, the Philippines, China, Japan, and the major cities of Europe. Once again inspired by her surroundings, her travels, and her in-depth study of the music of India, Lily produced a number of works such as "Songs of Ind," "From a Caravan," "Moroccan Mosaics," "From a Sufi's Tent," and "Himalayan Sketches." Further study of the musical traditions of India also led to a keen interest in Indian dance as an expression of the country's legends and history. She grasped the Indian custom of depicting their spiritual life through the drama and power of their music and dance. This led to a collaboration with dance teacher Helen Frost, resulting in "Oriental and Character Dances," a beautifully illustrated work published in 1930. A famous Indian poet and philosopher, Sir Rabindranath Tagore, expressed his praise of Mrs. Anderson by writing that he didn't "understand how an American woman can have so much understanding and sympathy for our people."

In an interview for *Better Homes and Gardens* magazine she spoke of the origin of another of her enduring favorites, "My Love is a Fisherman." "That, I wrote one dawn in India. We were on a slow train crossing over the Ganges on a trestle, on our way back to Calcutta. The light was still faint in the eastern sky and, in the silence of the newborn day, scores of red-sailed fishing boats were going out to sea. I was stirred and inspired by the sight, and began to write on the margin of a magazine I held." When her husband inquired what she was doing, she replied that she was writing a song, "and by the time we had again reached land the song was complete, words and music, marked all over the magazine!"

Lily pursued other creative outlets beyond her music, writing music criticism and travel articles. Her scholarly interest in art, history, architecture, philosophy, religion, and native customs are evident in her prose. Her subjects ranged from Indian architecture to snake charmers and devil-dancing to the rhythmic prayers of Ceylon, and her articles appeared in magazines such as *Etude, Musical Quarterly, Dance, Calcutta Review, World Traveler,* and *Architect and Engineer.* In addition to her achievements as a composer she is considered a poet of distinction. She published many sonnets and wrote the lyrics for nearly all of her songs. This ability to successfully write both the composition and the words to accompany it are rare in the realm of music. "Music and words come to me together—a body and soul proposition, I call it." She also found the time to paint and supplied the cover illustrations for much of her published sheet music, displaying a talent for watercolors.

During this productive creative period, Lily Strickland sometimes used male pseudonyms for her compositions. George Gershwin and Irving Berlin were garnering lots of attention as a dynamic composer/songwriter team of popular music, and Igor Stravinsky was challenging the classical music tradition of the day. It was a male-dominated field, but Lily did not shy away from a determined focus on her chosen career. Although she never outwardly expressed concern that her music would not be taken seriously during this time of prejudice against female composers, she took the pen names of Homer Cloud, Terence O'Shea, and

Michael DeLongpre, among others. In this way she ignored the discrimination of her day, worked diligently, and tactfully sidestepped the problem. On one occasion she even used her mother's name, Teresa Hammond, spelled backwards as Aseret Dnommah, suggesting an Indian name as the composer of "A Beggar at Love's Gate." Lily was known to have a delightful sense of humor, and perhaps this is one example of her amused riposte.

In fact her recognition as an important composer was beginning to grow despite any professional gender bias. In 1924 her alma mater, Converse College, conferred a Doctor of Music degree on her. Her southern and bayou songs were being performed by famous concert artists such as Galli-Curci, Paul Robeson, Burl Ives, Lawrence Tibbet, and Rosa Ponselle. Especially popular was "Mah Lindy Lou," and its universal appeal was expressed by the *Raleigh News & Observer,* "the lilting and haunting saga of the mockingbird singing . . . in the moonlight does something elemental and noble to the flintiest among us. It is hard to hear 'Mah Lindy Lou' without thinking of youth and love, of the richness and variety of summer nights." Another newspaper account related how, with a twinkle of amusement in her eye, Mrs. Strickland told of hearing a great prima donna singing it, imposing an Italian accent on the Negro dialect; and how yet another diva's German accent made it impossible to understand a word she sang. In addition to its performance around the world, seven recordings were made under the Columbia and Victor labels. Other accolades followed. Another work from her time in India, "The Cosmic Dance of Siva," was performed successfully in New York by acclaimed dancer Ted Shawn. In 1930 her oratorio "St. John the Beloved" was performed at the Spartanburg, South Carolina, Music Festival and by the Rotoli Choral Club in Atlanta with great success. The Atlanta Constitution lauded it as a work "that is not only a masterpiece, but is uplifting in spirit." Other notable ensembles such as the New York Philharmonic and the Metropolitan Opera Orchestra also performed her work. Her Christmas cantata "Star Over Bethlehem," and another cantata, "The Song of David," garnered immediate attention and continue to be used widely today in churches of various denominations.

In 1930 the Andersons returned to the United States and settled in the artists' colony of Woodstock, New York, in the Catskill Mountains, enjoying a complete contrast to their life in the tropics of India. Later they moved to Great Neck, Long Island. They also traveled to Charleston, South Carolina, in 1942, where they spent eight months while Mr. Anderson set up a U.S.O. (United Service Organization) Club. Lily was intrigued by the atmosphere and charm of the historic city and again translated that experience into music, an orchestral suite in six parts called "Charleston Sketches." It included "The Bells of St. Michael's," "On the Battery," and "Old House on Tradd Street." The suite for strings was arranged by Tony Hadgi and received its premiere performance by the Charleston String Symphony, and later was performed as originally written for full orchestra by the Charleston Symphony Orchestra.

The *Charleston News and Courier* also noted that an important part of Lily Strickland's work "lies in her valuable contribution to the field of music education. She has composed volumes of part songs for children of all grades; operettas, pantomimes and dances. Many schools use her volumes of part songs for children." Lily believed that music education should be included in the schools' regular curricula—not a readily accepted idea for educators at the time. She felt strongly that it was vital to develop creativity in children and that the performing arts were a key instrument in achieving this. It was a recurring theme in her writings and in her own contributions to the musical field with pieces written for children, many of which continue to be used for educational purposes today. Another subject that often appeared in her magazine articles was the lack of encouragement and recognition for American composers within their own country. She thought that too much emphasis was placed on training abroad among young American musicians and composers. She felt that Europe could provide additional stimulation as well as valuable perspective, "but they must live and feel America in order to compose American music."

In 1948 Lily and Courtenay Anderson retired to a twenty-six-acre estate they called "Arcady" in the Blue Ridge Mountains near Hendersonville, North Carolina. Lily continued to compose and write, remaining creative and active over the next ten years until her death from a stroke on June 6, 1958. She is buried next to her husband in Anderson's Silverbrook Cemetery. In a humble expression of her thankfulness for the talents she had received during her life, she requested that her tombstone read "He put a song in my heart."

Lily Strickland Anderson's prolific career numbers 395 songs, piano works, cantatas, anthems, choral ensembles, and operettas as well as music for the Ziegfeld Follies and other well-known dance groups published by thirty-seven different music companies. Her other creative achievements include more than one hundred articles and poems. Her husband's loving tribute at her funeral concluded, "Her poems and musical compositions disclose how delicately her heart and mind were attuned to the rhythm and beauty of life. She had an enthralled conception of the universe around her which inspired rare artistic expression." Her contribution as an American-born and educated composer is remarkable still for her ability to capture and echo the spirit of early-twentieth-century America.

SEPTIMA POINSETTE CLARK

1898-1987

Educator and Civil Rights Activist

IT WAS A FRIDAY NIGHT IN JULY 1959, AND SEPTIMA CLARK was just wrapping up the final session of a series of workshops she taught at the Highlander Folk School in Monteagle, Tennessee. The workshop attendees were beginning to watch a documentary film entitled *The Face of the South*. Highlander's director, Myles Horton, was away for the evening. All of a sudden the doors flew open and eighteen law enforcement officers plus a reporter and photographer from the *Chattanooga Free Press* burst into the auditorium. They informed Septima that they had a search warrant for liquor on the premises. (Highlander was located in a dry county.) Unrattled, Septima told them, "Just go in that kitchen and look all over. You won't even find cooking sherry in there." After turning up nothing in the main hall and other buildings, they entered the locked basement of Horton's home, where they claimed to find several bottles of whiskey. Since Myles and Septima were always on guard for a possible raid, they later suspected the liquor had been planted. Septima and three men were taken into custody and locked up in the county jail. Before being freed on bail, she spent several hours

Septima Clark worked tirelessly to improve the lives of African Americans through education and civil rights activism.

in a rank cell where waste from the men's room above ran down the walls.

Everyone involved on both sides knew the raid was a ruse, trumped up to close the influential and controversial Highlander Folk School. It was a training ground for people from across the country to lead black voter registration drives and other desegregation activities—extremely radical actions for anywhere in the country but especially so in the rural South. The integrated school was labeled "the center of Communism in the South" and was threatened constantly with being shut down. Drawing on her inner strength, Septima returned to Highlander and continued her work even more determined to help the cause succeed.

Septima was born May 3, 1898, to Peter Porcher Poinsette and Victoria Warren Anderson, the second of eight children. Her father was a former slave on Casa Bianca plantation, outside of Charleston, owned by Joel Poinsette. (Poinsette was the former U.S. ambassador to Mexico and a botanist who brought the bright-red plant home that became known as the "poinsettia" so widely popular at Christmastime today.) Septima's mother, the daughter of an American Indian father and Haitian mother, had been raised in Haiti, where she received a rigorous European education. Victoria's education and her "free issue" status instilled a sense of confidence in the young woman. Peter, freed after the Civil War, went to work for the Clyde Steamship Line, traveling between New York and Miami. On one of his ship's stops, he met Victoria, who was then living in Jacksonville, Florida, and they married and settled in Charleston. In later years, Septima would describe her father as a "gentle, tolerant man who knew how to make the best of a situation" and her mother as "fiercely proud" and quick to make it known that she had never been a slave. As a parental role model, Victoria was notably unintimidated by the racial prejudice displayed toward blacks and taught her children to have courage in the face of it. Septima recalled that "she wanted you to be able to stand your ground, regardless of where you were or whatever happened." The character traits of both of her parents would shape Septima and serve her well in the years ahead.

The Poinsettes valued education and sent Septima to a small private school for African-American children, taught in the two-room home of a local black matron. Tuition was one dollar a month and the pupils were "selected" among those whom the teacher considered a part of the upper caste of the black population. Proper decorum was demanded and a sense of pride was expected. By the fourth grade, Septima entered the public school system and attended a segregated school for black children but was taught by a white teacher. By law, black teachers could not teach black children in public schools, so the white teachers taught black children and white children in separate buildings. The black children soon learned not to speak to their teachers on the street after school, because the teacher, embarrassed about her situation, would have them whipped. For Septima, this was a hard lesson and an injustice that she sought to rectify in early adulthood.

By the end of the ninth grade, Septima wanted to leave school to work to help her parents support the family, but her mother insisted that she further her education at the Avery Normal Institute. Avery, founded in 1865, was the only college-preparatory school in Charleston for African Americans. Upon her graduation in 1916, Septima's instructors, recognizing her love of learning, pushed her toward college, specifically Fisk University in Tennessee. Her parents were supportive of this idea, but in reality they, as well as Septima, knew that the tuition of $19.00 a month was out of reach. Avery's tuition of $1.50 a month had been difficult enough for the family to afford, so Septima, as much as she wanted to go, argued against attempting it. Instead she turned her attention to finding employment as a teacher in Charleston.

It was challenging to find a position because the Charleston public schools still did not hire African Americans, but blacks were allowed to teach on the sea islands surrounding the city. With the help of her local church minister, she was able to get a job teaching at Promise Land School at the southern end of Johns Island. The population of Johns Island was overwhelmingly African American, descendants from slaves brought over from Africa and the Caribbean to work on the island's numerous plantations. The island was still agricultural and rural, reached only by ferry and largely isolated from the outside world. The black residents spoke Gullah, the language derived from a mix of African, French, and English words, and school attendance was directly affected by the harvest and the weather. The older children didn't come to school until after the harvest in November, and a rainy day meant greater numbers of students, most of whom would disappear if the weather cleared. The children were happy, however, to escape working in the fields to go to school even if it meant paddling across creeks or walking in the mud for many miles. Even Septima suffered from the walk to the schoolhouse, developing frostbite on her feet that first winter. Septima and one other teacher divided 132 pupils in a two-room, log schoolhouse. The only light came from the windows, which had no panes of glass or screens, only shutters to close against the wind and cold. A central fireplace was the sole source of heat for both rooms. Septima taught the fourth through the eighth grades finding a wide difference in the educational levels of her pupils. Initially she had no blackboard and used paper dry cleaner bags on which to write stories and tack them up on the wall. The children had no desks, only benches with no backs. When writing they knelt beside the bench on the floor so that they could use it as a table top. In these primitive conditions Septima devised a method of teaching by getting the children to tell stories about their surroundings and their everyday life. She wrote them on the bags and taught them the basics of reading and writing through their own stories. These were written as spoken in the native Gullah, although she guided them toward the English words simultaneously.

All this effort was compensated with a salary of $35 a month. In contrast the white teacher teaching across the road with only a handful of white students received $85 a month. Even in this rugged setting, Septima found that she loved teaching, and she employed her natural talents as a patient and kind mentor who strove to encourage learning and self-esteem. Before long the parents of Septima's pupils sought out her help too since most of them had had very little education. She began teaching night classes, which adults attended after long days in the fields. From this first teaching experience Septima would create and develop the techniques she used throughout her lifelong teaching career: She tapped into the rich oral tradition of the children and adults as the starting ground for their reading and writing; she drew out and respected the individual skills and experience that each of her students possessed; and in a practical approach she taught them to trace the outlines of written words to practice their cursive writing. She later reflected on this time with the "John's Island folk" as a confirmation of her childhood dream of "teaching the poor and underprivileged of my own underprivileged race."

In 1919 Septima accepted a teaching job at her alma mater, Avery Normal Institute. She also joined the NAACP and participated in its drive to change the state law that didn't allow black teachers in the majority of public schools. As a volunteer she helped collect signatures of more than ten thousand people in support of the change. This first grassroots political effort was successful in convincing the legislature; in 1920 black teachers were allowed to teach in the city of Charleston for the first time.

At the same time, Septima, who had had little opportunity for any social life, met a navy cook named Nerie Clark. Although they had only spent a few days together on a couple of occasions, they decided to marry, against her parents' objections. The marriage did not go well. Nerie was often away at sea, and Septima had to endure alone the loss of their first child, who died shortly after she was born. After Nerie's discharge from the navy, they moved to Dayton, Ohio, where their second child was born. She soon learned that her husband's absences were due to another reason: He had a mistress. Nerie asked Septima to leave Dayton. Stunned by this revelation, she left, and she and her infant son were taken in by Nerie's family in Hickory, North Carolina. Ten months later she got word that her husband was dying from kidney disease. She traveled back to Dayton in time to say good-bye, and she brought his body home for burial. Demonstrating her compassion and strength of character, she "pieced together all the sweet notes he had written me, so the minister could help the family feel good" at the funeral. Although she was able to put aside the hurt and anger, she vowed never to marry again.

In 1926 Septima returned to Johns Island to teach, finding slightly improved conditions such as the addition of outdoor privies and a covering of creosote painted on the building to help stop the drafts. But she struggled to care for her young son on her meager salary and with the many demands on her time. After he suffered through a serious childhood illness, she finally decided that it would be best to send him back to his grandparents in Hickory for proper care. She visited as often as she could, but Nerie Jr. would be raised by his father's family until adulthood. Septima, in an effort to improve her opportunities, moved to Columbia, South Carolina. She found the capital city to be much more open to African Americans than Charleston, and she attended her first interracial meetings of various civic organizations there. Blacks were still segregated to their own seating section but were included in the activities, and this provided Septima with more training in organizing and fund-raising.

She also became involved in the effort of another teacher, J. Andrew Simmons, to equalize the pay between black teachers and white teachers. She helped gather records for the court case showing that the black teachers usually received about half of what the white ones were paid. With the NAACP's backing and the work of one of their lawyers, Thurgood Marshall (who later became a major civil rights advocate and the first African-American Supreme Court Justice), the case went before the federal court. In 1945 Judge Waring from Charleston ruled that equally qualified black and white teachers had to receive equal compensation. In response, the school authorities implemented a test, the National Teachers Exam, which all the teachers had to pass. Some resigned rather than attempting the test, but Septima earned an A and her salary immediately doubled. Throughout this quest for equal pay, Septima pursued her college degree in summer school and through extension courses. She attended Columbia University in New York and Atlanta University to broaden her teaching skills, studying under W.E.B. DuBois, considered the greatest black intellectual of the time. Reaching another personal goal, Septima was awarded a Bachelor of Arts degree from Benedict College in Columbia, South Carolina, in 1942. With three more summers of work she attained her master's degree from Hampton Institute at Hampton, Virginia.

After eighteen years in Columbia, Septima went back to Charleston to help care for her elderly mother. She also became involved in civic activities there as well, raising funds for the Tuberculosis Association, which she helped to integrate through her personable approach and dedicated manner. She became chairman of the YMCA board and found herself in the mayor's office one day to ask for his assistance. Two other colleagues, both white women, accompanied her. The mayor seated the two women across from him with his back to Septima. She calmly sat behind him and began to plead her case. Although the other women were distressed by the obvious discrimination, Septima was determined to not let anything keep her from the purpose of their visit. The mayor agreed to Septima's requests, and she learned that "having patience and seeing things from the long view, and not permitting myself the costly luxury of losing my temper" could reap results.

Septima, at the urging of another teacher, went to the Highlander Folk School in the summer of 1953. Under the leadership of Myles Horton and his wife, Zilphia, a white couple, the school was beginning to make inroads in the course of the civil rights movement. Septima found the workshops stimulating and exhilarating. They were designed to ponder problems of segregation and then respond with decisive action. At the end of every session, each person was asked what they individually were going to do to address the problem when they got home. Horton encouraged Septima and invited her to return often. She spent the next couple of summers there helping to write school pamphlets, such as *A Guide to Action for Public School Desegregation*. She also recruited and encouraged several other future leaders such as Esau Jenkins, from Johns Island, and Rosa Parks, who made her famous stance by not giving up her seat on the bus in Montgomery, Alabama.

But all was not to proceed without more setbacks in her life. After the *Brown vs. Board of Education* decision in 1954 desegregating public schools, the local authorities in South Carolina fought against the ruling. South Carolina public schools required all teachers to fill out a form listing the organizations that they belonged to, and the legislature passed a law that no city or state employee could be a member of the NAACP. This meant that Septima, who had taught for forty years, was dismissed without explanation and found herself at sixty years old without a job or a pension. She attempted to convince the other black teachers who had either resigned from the NAACP or hidden their affiliation that they must unite to fight against the law. She signed and sent out 726 letters asking them to stand up for their rights. She considered it the big failure of her life that she was unable to motivate more than a handful of them to act. When they approached their supervisor they were told they were simply ahead of their time. Even at home Septima met with disapproval as her brother expressed the family's frustration that she would give up her good job and that they couldn't understand why she couldn't just be like everybody else.

Soon after these events, Myles Horton offered Septima a paid position as the education director for Highlander. Septima moved there and embraced the opportunity to put all her years of teaching, civic organization, and political activism to use. She developed workbooks for adults that provided practical information, with chapters including "Political Parties in South Carolina," "Social Security," and "Taxes You Must Pay in South Carolina."

Then Esau Jenkins from Johns Island pointed out the need to prepare people in their own local community with the preparation needed to register to vote. Prior to the Voting Rights Act of 1965, reading and writing skills were required to answer a series of sometimes quite arbitrary questions to attain a voter registration card. Horton, Clark, and Jenkins brought a group of island residents to Highlander for training and then loaned them funds to establish a place on the island to hold local classes. A co-op grocery store was located in the front of the building with the classes held in two rooms in the back. The store not only helped to raise money to repay the loan but also camouflaged the activities in the rear. The literacy lessons were focused on civic responsibility and led to many blacks registering and voting. The idea of Citizenship Schools was born and quickly spread to other communities. Their success fanned the flames of the accusations of Communist activity at Highlander finally culminating in the raid in 1959. In February 1960 the school lost its charter on the basis that it was running a racially integrated school in direct violation of Tennessee law. Myles Horton fought back but lost his appeal in April 1960.

Anticipating this outcome, Horton had already begun to join forces with the Southern Christian Leadership Conference (SCLC). Martin Luther King Jr. and other SCLC organizers were impressed with Highlander's work and recognized Septima Clark's contribution of increasing black voter registration and her talent of fostering leadership. In 1961 she became the director of education and teaching for the SCLC under Andrew Young. They located their Citizenship School program at Dorchester, a former church retreat near the coast of Georgia. In those peaceful surroundings, Septima oversaw the training of local leaders who in turn went back to their towns across the South to teach others how to read and write and, subsequently, register to vote, vote, and even participate in peaceful protest. By the spring of 1961, eighty-two trained teachers were holding citizenship classes in Alabama, Georgia, South Carolina, and Tennessee. Septima also began traveling all over the South, visiting her teachers and recruiting new ones.

By this time the segregationists had escalated their threats, harassment, and destruction of property into physical attacks against the activists and sympathizers. Septima and her teachers were targets, and many of her colleagues endured injury and beatings. A church in Grenada, Mississippi, where she and her trainees had just met, was set on fire minutes later. Countless other interested people lost their jobs just by attending one of the citizenship meetings. Despite these oppressive circumstances, 897 Citizenship Schools were operating between 1957 and 1970. Later Septima remembered Young saying that the Citizenship Schools were the base on which the whole civil rights movement was built. Although she did not always see eye to eye with many of the leaders of the movement, she became known as the SCLC's "mother conscience" and earned their respect for her selfless dedication and grounded focus. She was fully supportive of Dr. King's push for civil disobedience in a peaceful, nonviolent manner. Several times Dr. King visited at her home in Charleston, and she was one of the small group invited to accompany him to Norway to accept the 1964 Nobel Peace Prize. As the movement grew and attracted more militant young people, she worked to counter their violent approach. On one occasion she attempted to convince Stokely Carmichael, leader of the Black Power Boys, to drop their violent tactics. Some years later he recognized her as the "one who got me to realize that being violent was the one thing that I shouldn't do."

Even after the devastating loss of Dr. King in 1968, Clark continued her work with the SCLC until her retirement in 1970. She settled back in Charleston but continued to get involved in causes close to her heart. Quietly proud of her life's accomplishments for civil rights, she felt that women had been overlooked for leadership opportunities to the detriment of the movement. She adopted the cause of women's rights, joining the National Organization for Women (NOW) and campaigning for the Equal Rights Amendment. She raised money for black student scholarships, helped organize day care centers, and became a member of the same school board that had fired her for her NAACP membership.

Septima garnered recognition for her achievements from many national groups. The SCLC held a banquet in her honor at the Francis Marion Hotel in Charleston, presenting her the Martin Luther King Jr. award "for Great Service to Humanity." In 1976 the National Education Association gave her its Race Relations Award, and in 1979 she received the Living Legacy award at a White House ceremony from President Jimmy Carter. By legislative act a Charleston roadway was named the Septima P. Clark Expressway in 1978. Other South Carolina accolades followed with the Order of the Palmetto, the highest civilian award of the state, and the Wil Lou Gray Award of the South Carolina Gerontological Society.

Septima Clark died at the age of eighty-nine in a Johns Island nursing home.

GERTRUDE SANFORD LEGENDRE

1902–2000

Adventurer

TWELVE-YEAR-OLD GERTIE SANFORD COULDN'T SLEEP. How could she when renowned hunter/photographer Paul Rainey was in the house and about to show his films of lion hunting in Africa! Her parents were having a party to honor him, and after dinner he would be sharing his experiences with their guests. She had been put to bed at seven but had lain awake listening for the sounds of the table clearing downstairs. Finally, she heard movement, and she quietly slipped past the nanny's door and eased down the stairs just far enough to peek through the banister rails into the living room. She later recounted: "There it was: Africa in jumpy, badly lighted, black-and-white images against the far wall. I may have had a poor seat, but that evening changed my life. From that moment on, I knew that I would go to Africa someday."

Born in 1902 in Aiken, South Carolina, Gertie was the youngest of John and Ethel Sanford's three children. Most of the year, the Sanfords lived near Albany, New York, in Amsterdam, where Mr. Sanford ran the family carpet business. His time was divided

Gertrude Sanford is accompanied by (left to right) Donald Carter, curator of Mammals for the American Museum of Natural History; Morris Legendre; and her future husband, Sidney Legendre, on a hunting expedition in Abyssinia for the museum in 1928. They are pictured with a giant mountain nyala, one of a group they collected that is still on exhibit at the museum.

between managing the carpet business and his passion for his horse-breeding farm called Hurricana. Mrs. Sanford was a distant cousin of her husband and the daughter of Henry Shelton Sanford, a businessman and diplomat who served as ambassador at large to St. Petersburg, Russia; Paris, France; and Brussels, Belgium. He was widely traveled, and some say Gertie inherited her love of travel from her maternal grandfather. She also was named for his wife, Gertrude Ellen du Puy, whom he met while in Belgium. Gertie's paternal grandfather, Stephen Sanford, had built the carpet business into the largest carpet manufacturer in the state of New York. Her father served several terms in the House of Representatives before taking over the company at the age of forty.

Growing up in a privileged household meant moving around with the change of the seasons. Generally the Sanfords spent August through December in Amsterdam, New York. After Christmas they traveled south to Aiken, South Carolina, well established as a winter home for northern horse breeders, riders, hunters, and polo players. When the weather got hot, the family would summer in Maine or Newport, Rhode Island. Other summers they would sail to France or England where Mr. Sanford kept racehorses. Gertie was educated by tutors until she applied to Foxcroft School in Middleburg, Virginia. The two-year-old school had already made a name for itself as one of the finest girls' schools of the day, but Gertie's application was turned down due to lack of space in her class. She promptly wrote back to the founder, Miss Charlotte Noland, that she would "sleep in a bath-tub if need be," earning herself a place there and teaching her the value of tenacity.

After her graduation from Foxcroft in 1920, Gertie made a choice that would set the tone for the rest of her life. Most young women of means would enter the social whirl of debutante parties, balls, and teas, all part of the search for a proper husband. Instead, Gertie chose to go out west on a camping trip to the Grand Tetons in Wyoming to hunt elk. She was invited by an old friend, Tom Evans, and accompanied by her father's personal secretary, Dr. Henry Coffin, and a guide. Raised around horses and the sporting life outdoors, she embraced the rustic experience of the trip with the pack ponies, log fires, and sleeping under the stars in the cold clear nights. She shot her first elk and, although the animal was not especially remarkable, she was ecstatic about her success. Later she recalled:

. . . if I hadn't gone on that first trip to the Tetons, I might never have known the thrill of life in the wilderness. If I hadn't begun to travel, I might never have known how much there was to see and to learn. Half the battle is opportunity. The other half is the willingness to say "yes."

Over the next seven years Gertie went on many other hunting and fishing trips in the wildernesses of Alaska, Canada, New Brunswick, and the Laurentians. Often her brother, Laddie, went along, as well as Evans and Coffin. More adventures followed as they pursued moose, caribou, and Alaskan brown bear. Between travels, Gertie returned to her family home then in Manhattan, where the Roaring Twenties were in full swing. Her parents often entertained and hired the leading entertainers and orchestras of the day for dances in the upstairs ballroom of their grand home. They even hosted a dinner party for the Prince of Wales in the summer of 1924. In perfect contrast to her rugged outdoor camp trips, Gertie's days in Manhattan were filled with tennis, polo, and tea parties, and nights with more parties, dinner dances, theater, and balls. She and her sister, Janie, spent a summer on the French Riviera rubbing elbows with the American artists, writers, and actors flocking there, such as Ernest Hemingway, F. Scott Fitzgerald, John Dos Passos, and Harpo Marx. Not one to take herself too seriously, she described that time as "simple-minded nonsense and a lot of fun."

Then, one day at the Saratoga race track back home in New York, family friends Harold and Peggy Talbott asked Laddie and Gertie to go on safari with them to Africa. The brother and sister jumped at the chance and set out on the arduous journey in December. The only realistic mode of transportation for making the trip at that time was crossing the Atlantic by ship, changing to another in the Mediterranean, and then steaming on through the Indian Ocean to the port of Mombasa. The sea journey took them eighteen days, and Gertie suffered from seasickness the whole time, as she always did when at sea. Next was rail travel overland from Mombasa to Nairobi, Kenya. All in all it took more than a month to get there, and then once in Nairobi, they still needed more time to equip themselves for the safari. In 1927 there was no central place from which to order supplies, so they estimated what they would need and purchased canned goods, medicines, and camping gear wherever they could find it. Four-wheel drive vehicles were also not available, so they bought two trucks and two sedans. Two guides and a large number of Africans were hired to spot the game, set up the camp, and deal with the animals that they killed. They rose before dawn each day, jostling and bumping across the plains for miles and miles, searching for game. In the evenings they returned to camp where they sat on folding camp chairs and passed around the quinine bottle to ward off malaria. After supper around the fire they would recount their day and plan the next until they each retired to their tents. They slept on cots surrounded by netting to screen themselves from mosquitoes, which were as large as moths. They saw thousands of animals—ostrich, warthog, giraffe, gazelle, impala, wildebeest, zebra, lion, *mbogo* (buffalo), and elephant. For Gertie the feeling of remoteness from city life provided a time for reflection. She was far, far away "from the routine of social life—weddings, parties, polo, fancy clothes and repetitious, trite, silly talk." She remembered thinking that she "would like to stay forever in that open land with its strange night sounds and smells."

After shooting lion, mbogo, and elephant, they began their long trip home in early March. Feeling sadness at parting with their guides who had led them safely and competently through Kenya, Tanganyika, and Uganda, Gertie knew that "the atmosphere of Africa had delivered its magic in a very real way; Africa was in my blood" and that she would return. She also knew that she wanted to hunt in other countries around the world and that her future trips would have a different objective; perhaps she could gather specimens for a museum collection.

After her return to New York, Gertie decided to approach the American Museum of Natural History's president, Fairfield Osborn, with a proposal. She realized that the museum lacked specimens of a certain Abyssinian antelope in their collection. She also knew that museums were quite competitive about their exhibits at that time and hoped to appeal to more and more people by including the rarest and most unusual exhibits in their collections. Dr. Osborn, a bit taken aback by this bold plan from a young aristocratic woman, explained that it would require a minimum of thirty thousand dollars just to mount the exhibit. After hunting the animals, they would have to be reconstructed perfectly using only the skeletons and skins. The setting for the exhibit had to be recreated from the wild, incorporating the grasses, trees, and plants as well. Photographs and sketches would need to be made of the background scenery so that it could later be painted by an artist for the exhibit. Gertie was discouraged by this large sum in addition to what would be needed to outfit the trip. Not being one to give up easily, she pondered what to do next. She decided to gather her courage and ask her father for the money. With the size of the monetary request and the rigors and danger involved for his daughter, he had every reason to say no. Gertie figured her best plea was to ask if he would like to give her a present equal to the polo ponies that he had given Laddie. At first he was silent, but after she extolled the value that the exhibit would have to the public and how eager she was to attempt it, he agreed.

Excitedly she began preparations to make the trip the following winter. She telegraphed her friends Morris and Sidney Legendre, brothers she had met in England, to join her on this adventure. Donald Carter, curator of Mammals for the museum would go too. There was some European colonization of Abyssinia, or Ethiopia, but for the most part it was considered very backward even by

African standards at the time; Ethiopian emperor Haile Selassie had traveled to Europe and had reestablished diplomatic ties with the United States, hoping to bring his country into the twentieth century without sacrificing its ancient culture.

Another difficult trip by slow, bumpy train brought Gertie's expedition climbing into the interior of the country to Addis at an elevation of six thousand feet. They were invited to dine with the Emperor, and Gertie described the visit "like a page out of *The Arabian Nights*." Emperor Selassie was standing on a lion skin when he received them, and during dinner he was seated in a gold chair. The fourteen-course meal, which alternated between European and native fare, was served on dinner plates encrusted with gold coins. The native food consisted of cooked vegetables and various animal parts called *wat,* largely made from sheeps' brains and intestines. The Emperor conversed with Gertie in French and was shocked to learn that a woman would attempt wild game hunting. The party was invited to return on several occasions, and his Majesty even presented Gertie with a royal mule complete with a silver bit, red embroidered reins, and a green velvet saddle.

They spent nearly a month hiring the necessary staff such as cooks, trackers, and skinners and purchasing fifty mules to carry all the equipment needed for the four-month expedition. The entourage would average about twelve miles a day on foot, leaving before dawn and pitching camp midday. In the afternoon the hunters would scatter and shoot birds such as blue-winged geese, ibis, storks, and spur fowl until dark. Camp life was never dull as fights often broke out among the tribal staff, and activities as typically mundane as bathing proved a risky venture in murky waters full of crocodiles. Adding to the trials of the trip, some even contracted small pox and malaria. But they pressed on, and Gertie, Morris, and Sidney learned to lie in wait of dawn in their sleeping bags on different mountain tops to find the elusive nyala, or mountain antelope, that they sought for the museum. This was a successful tactic. Overall they collected over three hundred mammals and a hundred birds with the accompanying vegetation for the exhibition. The trip was successful in another way too as Gertie and Sidney became engaged.

The couple was married in New York City in September 1929, and a reception for hundreds of guests was held in the bride's fashionable and elegant family home at 9 East Seventy-Second Street. It was a lavish and proper affair, and Gertie thought that even her mother, who had died in 1924, would have approved. The honeymoon was a stark contrast but perfect for adventure-seekers. Gertie and Sidney took a pack trip into the Cassiar Mountains in British Columbia, stalking sheep and goats through snowdrifts and blizzards. After the trip they decided to drive down from New York through the southeast looking for a place to settle. Along the way they stopped at Dean Hall Plantation outside Charleston as the guests of Mr. and Mrs. Benjamin Kittredge Sr. After a morning duck hunt, Mr. Kittredge showed them the property next door called Medway Plantation. It dated back to the 1600s and had been at one time a prosperous rice plantation. When the Legendres saw it, the house was used as a weekend hunting camp and had fallen into disrepair. It had no electricity and no running water, but the faded brick house at the end of the avenue of moss-laden oaks half-concealed by the overgrown landscape captivated the couple. Gertie persuaded her father to help them buy it as their wedding present in the spring of 1930. They began renovating the main house and converted several other buildings on the property into guest cottages. Sidney dreamed of returning it to a working farm, trying to cultivate a series of crops and livestock—rice, barley, wheat, corn, cattle, and hogs. But eventually they had more success turning it into a tree farm, marketing pine timber from its large tracts of land. This afforded further work on the house and grounds and provided a comfortable lifestyle for them and, in time, their two daughters.

As much as they loved Medway, the call of travel was not abandoned. Every few years they set out on another expedition for a museum. They spent six months in 1932 in Indochina collecting for the American Museum of Natural History and three months in 1936 in southwest Africa for the Philadelphia Academy of Natural Sciences. Another outing for the Natural History Museum took them to Persia (Iran) in 1938.

But all this came to an end when World War II interrupted their lives. Sidney joined the navy and was sent to the Pacific in 1942, and Gertie went to Washington to get involved in the war effort. She got a job with the Office of Strategic Services (OSS), the predecessor to the CIA, working as a secretary handling sensitive and top secret war cables. The next year she was selected to go to the London office, working under Col. David Bruce and enduring food rationing, blackouts, and nearly constant German Luftwaffe bombing. On June 6, 1944, she was awakened by hundreds of Allied airplane motors roaring overhead as they headed to Normandy for the D-Day invasion. After the liberation of Paris that summer she was transferred there to work in the new OSS office. While waiting for renovations to be completed on the OSS headquarters, she was granted a five-day leave and found herself at odds. She ran into a friend, Bob Jennings, also on leave, and they concocted the idea of using the time off to get to the war front and back in five days. They thought that the war was about to end and on a lark they wanted to see it firsthand. On September 23, 1944, they set out driving a run-down car to cross the border several hours northeast of Paris. Just as they entered the town of Wallendorf they were pinned down by German snipers and faced surrender. Having quickly destroyed her OSS identity card as the Germans approached, Gertie assumed the role of a file clerk from the Paris embassy to protect herself from certain death.

Over the next six months Gertie was shuffled from one German prison to another, enduring interrogations, threats of death, and often primitive conditions. Hunger, filth, and boredom were ongoing daily companions. Basics like toilet paper, a cup of coffee, and bathing were scarce. At one point she was taken to Gestapo Headquarters in Berlin and then imprisoned for two months under twenty-four-hour guard. Moved yet again she joined a large group of former French generals, colonels, and diplomats all "Internes d'Honneur" in a hotel turned prison. The only other woman present was Madame Caillau, sister of Charles de Gaulle. Constant artillery pounding and bombing as Patton's Third Army approached the Rhine River gave her hope that the end of the war was near, but her imprisonment dragged on.

One day a Mr. Gay from the SS in Frankfurt drove up and told her of a secret plan to take her to a train that would cross the Swiss–German border at Konstantz. Suspicious of everyone, she doubted him, but he told her that he had made a promise (to whom she never found out) that he would help her escape. But if successful she must say that French not German assistance was given. After dark she walked to the railway station where she slipped onto the train and hid herself on the floor in the shadows between the seats. Slowly the train moved forward and then unexpectedly stopped 150 yards short of the border. Heart pounding, Gertie hesitated at the platform door, counting to sixty to gather her nerve to jump out and run to freedom. As she started to dash a German guard shouted for her to halt or be shot, but she kept running. As she reached the barrier gate shouting out "American Passport!" the Swiss guard raised it, granting her safety and freedom. The German border guard stopped just short on the other side, fuming in anger. She never knew why he didn't shoot as she ran away and always wondered if something had been arranged.

After the war she and Sidney returned to Medway and began the task of bringing it back again after the neglect of the years away. Their efforts garnered some international note when they founded the "Medway Plan" along with a retired economic consultant named William Bennett. They established a foundation to aid in the rehabilitation of Europe after the destruction of World War II. The City of Charleston adopted the French town of Fleurs de l'Orne, leading the way for 304 more European towns to have American counterparts helping to fund the restoration work on worthy structures and resettling nearly four thousand refugees.

By the summer of 1946 the couple began to seek another challenge. Dillon Ripley, associate curator of Zoology for the Peabody Museum of Natural History at Yale (and later the director of the Smithsonian), organized a trip for them to collect birds and mammals in Assam, India. One highlight of the trip was an invitation to visit the Maharajah of Cooch Behar (Bejar) in Calcutta. They stayed in his huge, pink, Victorian palace and learned of the young Raj's progressive plans for his country as England was turning it back over to self-rule. Then, shortly after their return home, Sidney suddenly died of a heart attack at the age of forty-seven. After a period of grief, Gertie reminded herself that she knew Sidney wouldn't have wanted her to give up their beloved Medway or stop living as they had done. She carried on by running the business of the plantation, dealing with the inevitable problems that arose on an estate of close to seven thousand acres. She even continued her travels, joining another of Dillon Ripley's expeditions for the Peabody Museum, this time to Nepal, where Dillon noted that she was the first white woman to see the south face of Mount Everest. She also ventured to Kathmandu (only the twenty-second European or American allowed to go) and was captivated by the "bright green valley surrounded by the snowy Himalayas—a legend, a dream vision from a poet's mind." Another trip for the American Museum of Natural History and the National Geographic Society took her to French Equatorial Africa and then on to the jungle of Gabon, where she visited Dr. Albert Schweitzer at his missionary hospital compound.

As the decades passed she divided her time between winters at Medway and summers at Fishers Island, New York, where she characteristically amazed her friends by swimming in the unbearably cold ocean every morning. She penned two autobiographical books, *The Sands Ceased to Run* (1947) and *The Time of My Life* (1987), chronicling her amazing and unconventional life. Her interest in the arts led to philanthropic endeavors hosted at Medway, often aiding local arts organizations such as the Carolina Art Association and the Charleston Symphony and providing temporary residence and studio space for many leading artists of the day.

In September 1989 she faced the devastation of Hurricane Hugo, whose winds snapped thousands of pine trees at Medway. Then in her late eighties, Gertie rallied to clear her land of more than six million board feet of timber sold at greatly discounted prices due to the flooded market from the hurricane's extended wrath. She also began replanting for the next generation, and, in that same spirit, in 1993 she established the Medway Environmental Trust, to preserve the property as a nature preserve for wildfowl and indigenous species, some of which were endangered. The house, surrounding buildings, and grounds would be made available to private groups and foundations for meetings and conferences. This thoughtful decision would lead to more land preservation on surrounding plantations helping to contain the encroachment of Charleston's urban sprawl.

Gertrude Sanford Legendre lived to see the new millennium before her death later that year on March 8 at Medway and, reflecting on her extraordinary experiences, summed up her philosophy on living: "I look ahead. I always have. I don't contemplate life, I live it, and I'm having the time of my life!"

BIBLIOGRAPHY

General Sources

Bodie, Idella. *South Carolina Women,* rev. and exp. ed. Orangeburg, S.C.: Sandlapper Publishing, Inc., 1991.

Edgar, Walter. *South Carolina: A History.* Columbia: University of South Carolina Press, 1998.

————, ed. *The South Carolina Encyclopedia.* Columbia: University of South Carolina Press, 2006.

Henrietta Dering Johnston

Forsyth, Alexander, ed. *Henrietta Johnston: Who Greatly helped . . . by drawing pictures.* Winston-Salem, N.C.: Museum of Early Southern Decorative Arts, 1991.

Mahler, Jane Gaston. "1708 Henrietta Dering Johnston*" in A Few Unsung Women: Colonial and Pioneer.* The National Historical Activities Committee of The National Society of the Colonial Dames of America, 1982.

Middleton, Margaret Simons. *Henrietta Johnston of Charles Town, South Carolina: America's First Pastellist.* Columbia: University of South Carolina Press, 1966.

Severens, Martha R. "Who Was Henrietta Johnston?" *The Magazine Antiques,* November 1995, 704–9.

Elizabeth Ann Timothy

Cohen, Hennig. *The South Carolina Gazette, 1732–1775.* Columbia: University of South Carolina Press, 1953.

Hirsch, Arthur Henry. *The Huguenots of Colonial South Carolina.* Columbia: University of South Carolina Press, 1999.

Wilder, Effie Leland. "1700 Elizabeth Timothy: America's First Woman Publisher" in *A Few Unsung Women: Colonial and Pioneer.* The National Historical Activities Committee of The National Society of the Colonial Dames of America, 1982.

Eliza Lucas Pinckney

Bellows, Barbara L. "Eliza Lucas Pinckney: Evolution of an Icon," *South Carolina Historical Magazine,* April/July 2005.

McLaughlin, J. Michael, and Lee Davis Todman. *It Happened in South Carolina.* Guilford, Conn.: The Globe Pequot Press, 2004.

Pinckney, Elise, ed. *The Letterbook of Eliza Lucas Pinckney.* Chapel Hill: The University of North Carolina Press, 1972.

Rogers, George Jr. *Charleston in the Age of the Pinckneys.* Columbia: University of South Carolina Press, 1980.

Ann Pamela Cunningham

Klosky, Beth Ann. "The Cry of 1853: Let's Save Mount Vernon." *Sandlapper Magazine,* August 1968.

Lesesne, Dr. J. Mauldin. "Ann Pamela Cunningham." *Distinguished Women of Laurens County.* Columbia, S.C.: The R. L. Bryan Company, 1972.

Sadler, Betty. "Ann Pamela Cunningham Saves Mount Vernon." *The State and The Columbia Record,* March 20, 1966.

Matilda Arabelle Evans

Beardsley, Edward H. *A History of Neglect: Health Care for Blacks and Mill Workers in the Twentieth-Century South.* Knoxville: The University of Tennessee Press, 1987.

Davis, Marianna W. *South Carolina's Black and Native Americans, 1776–1976.* Columbia, S.C.: State Human Affairs Commission, Bicentennial Project Editorial Board, 1976.

Evans, Matilda A. *Martha Schofield, Pioneer Negro Educator.* Columbia, S.C.: Dupre Printing Company, 1916.

Hine, Darlene Clark. "The Corporeal and Ocular Veil: Dr. Matilda A. Evans (1872–1935) and the Complexity of Southern History," *Journal of Southern History* 70.1 (February 2004): 3–34.

Sterling, Dorothy, ed. *We Are Your Sisters: Black Women in the Nineteenth Century.* New York: W.W. Norton & Company, 1984.

Tindall, George Brown. *South Carolina Negroes, 1877–1900.* Columbia: University of South Carolina Press (2003), ca. 1952.

Julia Mood Peterkin

Landess, Thomas, H. *Julia Peterkin*. Boston: G. K. Hall & Co., 1976.

Williams, Susan Millar. *A Devil and a Good Woman Too*. Athens: University of Georgia Press, 1997.

Laura Bragg

Allen, Louise Anderson. *A Bluestocking in Charleston: The Life and Career of Laura Bragg*. Columbia: University of South Carolina Press, 2001.

———. *Laura Bragg, A New Woman: Practicing Progressive Social Reform as a Museum Administrator and Educator*. PhD diss., University of South Carolina, 1997.

———. "Libraries and Museums: Laura Bragg's Free Library for Charleston" in *Humanities in the South 86*. Decatur, Ga.: Southern Humanities Council, 2000, 10–21.

Marie Cromer Seigler

Bedingfield, Susan, and Diane Palmer. "A Century of Service Equips 4-H for Future." *Clemson Extension Answers* 16.2 (Summer 2002).

Dickert, Margaret Anne. *Marie Samuella Cromer Seigler*. PhD thesis, University of South Carolina, 1988.

Griffin, Louise Huckabee. "Abbeville County Native Founder of 4-H Club Forerunner," *The Press and Banner and Abbeville Medium,* October 10, 1984.

Hamilton, L. C. "Canning Club Led to Bigger Things for Farm Women," *The News and Courier,* July 1, 1962.

Martin, O. B. *The Demonstration Work: Dr. Seaman A. Knapp's Contribution to Civilization,* 3rd ed. San Antonio, Tex.: Naylor, 1941.

Milner, Vivian. "Tomato Clubs Spread through Nation," *Aiken County Rambler,* November 13, 1980.

Reck, Franklin M. *The 4-H Story: A History of 4-H Club Work*. Ames, Iowa: National Committee on Boys and Girls Club Work and The Iowa State College Press, 1951.

Wessel, Thomas and Marilyn. *4-H: An American Idea, 1900–1980: A History of 4-H*. Chevy Chase, Md.: National 4-H Council, 1982, 14–16.

Wil Lou Gray

Henderson, Ellen. "Wil Lou Gray . . . Educator," *Sandlapper Magazine,* May 1975.

Montgomery, Mabel. *South Carolina's Wil Lou Gray: Pioneer in Adult Education, a Crusader, Modern Marvel.* Columbia, S.C.: Vogue Press, 1963.

Smith, George M. *The Opportunity Schools and the Founder Wil Lou Gray.* West Columbia, S.C.: Wil Lou Gray Opportunity School, 2000.

Lily Strickland Anderson

Howe, Ann Whitworth. *Lily Strickland: South Carolina's Gift to American Music.* Columbia, S.C.: The R.L. Bryan Company, 1970.

Kinscella, Hazel Gertrude. "An American Composer at Home," *Better Homes & Gardens* 16 (September 1937): 60, 94–97.

Rowland, Elizabeth. "Presenting Lily Strickland," *Sandlapper Magazine,* January/February 1975.

Walker, Cornelia G. *History of Music in South Carolina.* Columbia, S.C.: The R.L. Bryan Company, 1958.

Septima Poinsette Clark

Clark, Septima Poinsette, and Cynthia Stokes Brown. *Ready from Within: Septima Clark and the Civil Rights Movement.* Navarro, Calif.: Wild Trees Press, 1986.

Schiff, Karenna Gore. *Lighting the Way: Nine Women Who Changed Modern America.* New York: Miramax Books Hyperion, 2005.

Gertrude Sanford Legendre

Beach, Virginia Christian. *Medway.* Charleston, S.C.: Wyrick & Company, 1999.

Kittredge, Carola. "Charleston's Grandest Dame," *Town and Country,* April 1995.

Legendre, Gertrude Sanford. *The Time of My Life.* Charleston, S.C.: Wyrick & Company, 1987.

ABOUT THE AUTHOR

Native South Carolinian Lee Davis Perry was raised in Charleston and attended the University of Georgia, graduating with a degree in journalism and a minor in history in 1976. She pursued graduate work there in public relations, before beginning her advertising career in Atlanta. She worked for several large advertising agencies, among them J. Walter Thompson USA.

The pull of the ocean and the traditions of her childhood proved too strong to abandon for long though, and she returned to Charleston in 1987. She worked as a freelance advertising and marketing consultant on local and regional accounts before shifting gears to a writing career. In 1997 she joined J. Michael McLaughlin as coauthor of the *Insiders' Guide to Charleston,* one of The Globe Pequot Press's best-selling guidebooks in the Insiders' Guide series. They also coauthored a short collection of historical stories from the Palmetto State in Globe Pequot's *It Happened in South Carolina* (2003).

Succumbing to the allure of Charleston's Historic District, Lee has undertaken the renovation of an old house (ca. 1803) in the downtown peninsula area. Although it has been both a test of endurance and a labor of love, it provides a perfect setting to contemplate the interesting stories and players shaping South Carolina's colorful past.